IMAGES
of America

Naperville's Greene Barn and Oak Cottage

With a characteristic eye for detail and poignancy of touch, Margaret Barber Hipp (daughter of Harry H. Barber, cofounder of the Barber Greene Company) created this painting of the beloved Oak Cottage and the Greene barn. Overlooking the East Branch of the DuPage River, surrounded by lush prairie grasses, savannah and farmland and dominated only by the towering bur oaks on the property, the Greene family homestead nurtured several generations of the Greene family, starting from William Briggs Greene in 1842. (Courtesy of the Greene family.)

On the Cover: In this c. 1907 photograph are several Greene family members on the front porch of Oak Cottage enjoying the splendor of a late summer evening. A young couple appears to be in private conversation on the side porch. The porch was a place where the family would lounge after dinner or socialize with neighboring farm families on an evening stroll. (Courtesy of the Greene family.)

IMAGES
of America

NAPERVILLE'S GREENE BARN AND OAK COTTAGE

Revati Natesan
Foreword by Everett Trygve Brown

ISBN 978-1-4671-0830-0

Published by Arcadia Publishing
Charleston, South Carolina

Printed in the United States of America

Library of Congress Control Number: 2022934563

For all general information, please contact Arcadia Publishing:
Telephone 843-853-2070
Fax 843-853-0044
E-mail sales@arcadiapublishing.com
For customer service and orders:
Toll-Free 1-888-313-2665

Visit us on the Internet at www.arcadiapublishing.com

Contents

Foreword

I am honored to introduce *Naperville's Greene Barn and Oak Cottage*, a book about my family and its ancestral home. Although my last name is not Greene (but rather another color), I am one of the last living descendants of William Briggs Greene—who built the farmhouse near Naperville, Illinois, called Oak Cottage—to have the privilege of regularly staying in the historic home before it was vacated in 1983. My father, Thomas Brown, was the last person to grow up there, and I enjoyed many summer vacations and Christmases in my youth on the beautiful Greene farm visiting my lovely grandmother Grace Greene Brown. Just as generations before me, I sledded down the barn ramp in the winter; drove the old tractor around the farm in the summer; explored the, by then, eerily empty barn; and sipped lemonade on the porch while watching fireflies.

I was fortunately put in touch with the author, Revati Natesan, by a mutual friend in Naperville—Mary Lou Wehrli, whose heroic advocacy for the Greene farm I am eternally grateful for—and have since enjoyed liaising with and knowing her. I was delighted to learn of Revati's project, as I am proud of my pioneer family history and, like all my relatives, have exceptionally fond memories of Oak Cottage, which was the center of the universe for our clan for generations. I appreciate that Revati, who was already a well-accomplished contributor to the community, took such an interest in our family and its homestead and dedicated herself to tirelessly putting together this excellent work.

Since moving west to become early settlers of northeast Illinois in the 1830s and 1840s, the Greenes have been an illustrious and unusually close-knit family (the subject of several previous books and even a family newsletter!) and are well worthy of a new book for a broader audience, if I do say so myself. The family's venerable white house and colossal red barn still stand proudly where they have for more than a century and a half, even as their surroundings have changed beyond recognition, and they call for their story to be told to new generations.

With the perfect combination of treasured vintage photographs and fascinating history, *Naperville's Greene Barn and Oak Cottage* brings the past to life. It covers all the bases, from the early history of the area; the Greene family, with a special focus on W.B. Greene, the longtime family patriarch and renowned business and community leader; Oak Cottage and the barn; and the Greene family legacy to the area. Whether or not they had ever heard of the Greene farm, many readers will surely enjoy this book for years to come.

—Everett Trygve Brown

Acknowledgments

Writing a book on Naperville's Greene barn and Oak Cottage has been a journey more interesting and rewarding than I could have ever imagined. I want to especially thank and acknowledge a number of key individuals, without whom this book would not have been possible. With profound appreciation I thank Everett Trygve Brown, one of the last to have spent many summers at the Greene family homestead, for entrusting me with much material from his family archives. Many thanks to other members of the Greene family who dug deep into their family photo collection to find images for this book. Words cannot begin to explain how indebted I am to all of them, and also to those who gave me constructive feedback on the manuscript to make it complete.

Many thanks to all the tireless supporters who have been working with the Forest Preserve District of DuPage County to bring more attention to this cultural asset. I want to especially call out Mary Lou Wehrli, who along with her late husband, Herb Nadelhoffer (both descendants of farm families who settled in Naperville), has been instrumental in gathering community support across Naperville, Illinois, in a massive effort to spotlight and rescue the barn from ruin. A big thank-you to Rachel Jenness and others who have also been working with the Forest Preserve District of DuPage County to bring more attention to this significant landmark. Thank you to Caroline Finzer, a member of a five-generation Naperville family and a registered Girl Scout for 48 years, on her diligence in providing contact information.

I want to express my gratitude for the cooperation and assistance from Nichols Library, Jeanne Schultz, and Andrea Field from the Naperville Heritage Society; Daniel Hebreard and Johanna Biedron from the Forest Preserve District of DuPage County; Rick Collins from Trillium Dell Timber Works; and Becky and Bill Simon from Naperville Preservation Inc.

Thank you to my editor, Caroline Anderson, and the entire production team at Arcadia Publishing. I am grateful to Krish Natesan and our children for their help, patience, and understanding while I was working on the book.

Unless otherwise noted, all images are from the personal collection of the Greene family.

INTRODUCTION

The history of the Greene family homestead, comprising Oak Cottage and the big barn, is a window into the cultural heritage of America. For more than a century, hundreds of thousands of European immigrants from the New England and New York areas made their way to America's heartland, where they helped form the backbone of the nation's agricultural community. Rich glacial soils at the banks of the Great Lakes and rivers became readily available for settlement following the completion of the Erie Canal in 1825, Native American treaties, and preemption acts of Congress. Daniel Moon Greene, of English descent and born in 1807, was one of the early settlers who came to DuPage County, Illinois, in 1835. He acquired 250 acres of farmland at $3 an acre (east of the East Branch of the DuPage River) from the US government and became the first sheriff of the county. The ancestral records of Daniel Moon Greene date back to Lord Alexander de Greene de Boketon, the great-grandson of one of the Norman nobles who invaded England with William the Conqueror in 1066.

The fascinating story of the homestead began in 1842 when an early pioneer, William Briggs Greene, 23 years old at the time, came to DuPage County from Vermont. He had followed his uncle Daniel Moon Greene, helped him on the farm, and was able to save $1,000. He desired to own land and establish himself as a farmer, but by that time, all government land had been sold. He was able to negotiate with the widow of a neighboring farmer, the Goodrich family, and bought 200 acres of woodland (just west of the East Branch of the DuPage River) for $5 an acre. There was a tiny log cabin on the property in a grove of nine oak trees. William Briggs went back to Vermont to fetch his sweetheart, Harriet Elizabeth Meeker, in 1845. They lived in the log cabin for five years, where two of their six children were born. In 1850, William Briggs built a frame house close to the log cabin to accommodate his growing family. As the frame house was surrounded by nine oak trees, Harriet fondly christened their new home Oak Cottage. William Spencer Greene, son of William Briggs Greene, took over the management of the farm around 1882 and worked hard to expand and improve it. He constructed the barn, which notably contained the county's first wooden silo.

The history of a house becomes the history of a home, which in turn becomes the history of a family. The Greene family prospered, and the homestead at one time supported 16 people under its roof—babies, parents, grandparents, and hired men and women. Three Greene brides commenced their lives there. Three generations of the Greene family were raised at the homestead, while six generations sheltered there. The Greene family homestead is situated adjacent to Naperville, Illinois, in the Greene Valley Forest Preserve. It is a landmark on the south side of Hobson Road, which began as a rambling trail created by the footfalls of buffalo and Native Americans, between the East and West Branches of the DuPage River.

William Bertram Greene, a son of William Spencer Greene, made sure that the story of Oak Cottage would carry on. His guidance and business acumen left behind a legacy that contributes to the well-being of his progeny as well as mankind. At the present time, the Greene barn and Oak Cottage are owned by the Forest Preserve District of DuPage County, and as such, their future effectively depends on the public and its desire to preserve and utilize these venerable, historic structures today and for generations to come.

One

Presettlement Land and Life on the Midwest Prairie

Treat the earth well,
It was not given to you by your parents,
It was loaned to you by your children.

—Native American proverb

Early pioneers came to the United States from England, Germany, and France and settled along the East Coast of this new country. They were trying to liberate themselves from religious constraints and socioeconomic and political difficulties in their native countries. When they arrived, they found themselves competing for farmland, produce, and other necessities with people who were already here. This was the clarion call to go west and find new land on which to settle.

In the early 1800s, the region west of Michigan and Ohio was primarily a backwoods area, a wilderness with scattered footpaths created by Indigenous people and buffalo. These trails, located along watersheds and streams, provided a way westward through the wild country. In 1825, the Erie Canal opened up, providing a direct water route from Vermont and central New York via the Great Lakes to northern Illinois. The canal allowed settlers to travel westwards much more easily than the journey via land routes already in use by early pioneers, spurring the first great westward movement of early American settlers. Commerce, industry, and population saw unprecedented growth along its path, giving access to the country's rich hinterland. Town names such as Batavia, Geneva, and Oswego were widely duplicated, and the New England heritage was likewise transplanted.

When European settlers arrived in Illinois, they saw tall dense prairie grasses stretched before them for miles like waves of a great green sea. Dotting this continuous landscape of grasses and flowers were groves of oak and maple trees; it seemed as if the whole earth had been converted into green grass, blue sky, blossoming flowers, and glorious sunshine. They had never seen anything like this before. Some found it forbidding and were not sure that they would survive in this seemingly harsh environment. Others saw the promise of fertile land, independence, and opportunity.

At the time, much of the area surrounding the Great Lakes was occupied by the Illiniwek and Potawatomi Indian tribes. The Indians were eventually driven out west of the Mississippi, and the white settlers began the job of clearing the prairies grasses and thickets and establishing farms. In the 1830s, stagecoach routes radiating out of Chicago were established, with way stations in the area of the DuPage River watershed.

One can only imagine the exhilaration in the hearts of these passengers as they boarded the boat to be pulled by towpath mules through the Erie Canal to destinations out west, such as Cleveland, Detroit, and Chicago. A typical journey westward would start from New York, traverse the Erie Canal in a week, and then head to Buffalo, where passengers could board a ship to take them across Lake Erie to Cleveland or Detroit. The ship would then traverse Lake St. Claire and along the river onto Lake Huron, cross the Mackinac Strait, and finally reach Chicago. Enticed by dreams of land ownership and farming, some settlers would travel farther westward through 26 miles of wooded prairie land in covered ox wagons loaded with their family and belongings before they reached the fertile land that would become Naperville. (Both, Library of Congress.)

A group of Potawatomi Indians, including men, women, and children, pose above for a rare photograph taken in 1906. On the right are Chief Crane, a Potawatomi, holding a tomahawk, along with an unidentified Native American man. The word *Potawatomi* means "Keepers of the Sacred Fire," but they call themselves Neshnabek, which means "the True People." As keepers of the fire, the Potawatomi were in alliance with the Ottawa and Ojibwa tribes and had established several small settlements along rivers in the greater Chicago area, which they called Chicagoua or "wild onion." Seventeenth-century French traders were the first Europeans to have contacted the Potawatomi and to have written about them. The tribe was involved quite heavily in fur trade with the French and supplied them with raccoon, muskrat, and otter pelts. The tribe was even supportive of the settlers, but in 1803, as a result of frequent skirmishes and related deaths, the relationship quickly deteriorated. The Indian Removal Act of 1830 forced tens of thousands of Native Americans residing east of the Mississippi to relocate farther west. (Both, Library of Congress.)

This is the kind of scene that the settlers coming from the east encountered: rolling fields of tall prairie and small islands of woods. The pioneer farmers preferred the grassland to the wooded landscape for agricultural purposes, yet planted trees and cherished the wooded forests for building material and firewood. The Native Americans lived off of the bounty that the land produced. They revered the land, a spiritual relationship that had lasted for more than 10,000 years before the white settlers came. The sky was their father and the Earth their mother. (Photograph by Don Gardner.)

At left is a photograph of the Big Bluestem prairie grass. It can grow to be over six feet tall, has very deep root systems, and adapts to most well-drained soils. Native Americans had many uses for the plant, as it was a great substitute for rope used to tie down their dwellings. (Courtesy of the Forest Preserve District of DuPage County.)

T aerial photograph of the East Branch of the DuPage River shows the Greene barn and Oak Cottage at the southeast corner of Greene and Hobson Roads. The river is a 28-mile-long tributary of the Des Plaines River. Stephen J. Scott and his son Willard, while on a hunting trip in 1830, discovered the DuPage River south of present-day Naperville and built a cabin at the fork of the East and West Branches of the river in Will County. Other families soon arrived and chose areas around the river to build a homestead, farm, and raise their families. The proximity to water, the abundance of fish and bison, and the rich alluvial soil were all factors that helped them conquer the challenges of a new life in an unfamiliar place. (Courtesy of Mary Lou Wehrli.)

Pictured is the East Branch of the DuPage River. The river begins as two individual streams fed by copious springs. The East Branch, 25 miles long, begins in Bloomingdale and flows southward through 11 municipalities. The West Branch of the DuPage River, 35 miles long, starts in Schaumburg and continues southward through the entire county of DuPage. The two branches meet at Knoch Knolls Park in Naperville. The combined DuPage River continues southward from that point and empties into the Des Plaines River near Channahon, Illinois. (Photograph by the author.)

The first "plows" were often strong tree branches used to prepare the soil for farming, by turning and breaking up the soil, burying crop residues, and controlling weeds. In the early 1800s, farmers increasingly used a team of oxen or horses joined by a yoke to pull wooden plows, but seeds were still sown by hand. The plow was one of the most important agricultural implements utilized until John Deere invented the steel plow, which farmers used to clear fields of native plants. Farmers would use a team of two or more horses or oxen to pull the plows through the bumpy terrain. That was hard work for both man and beast to prepare prairie land for sowing and growing crops. With the invention of the internal combustion engine, farmers were able to plow land faster and cover more acreage in a day. (Both, Library of Congress.)

Shown is a rendering of Chief Black Hawk, known by his Sauk name as Ma-ca-tai-me-she-kia-kiak. He was a strong warrior and became an official war chief when his father died. He was proud of his native heritage and would defend it at all costs. He never accepted the treaty that surrendered Sauk lands to the American settlers, as the treaty was signed by three of his tribal chiefs who were drunk, under duress, and had no authority to do so. In 1832, when he was 65 years old, he led a group of some 1,000 Indians from the Sauk, Fox, and Kickapoo tribes and crossed the Mississippi River into Illinois to try to claim back land that they had loved and lost. (Library of Congress.)

Fort Payne was a trading post in Naper's Settlement, which was hastily fortified by Capt. Morgan L. Payne with a 100-foot-square stockade in 1831 in response to the settlers who feared violent attacks by Chief Black Hawk and the roaming Sauk Indians. The fort was spared from battle, but the Black Hawk War gave momentum to the US policy of Indian removal and forced Native American tribes to move west of the Mississippi. (Courtesy of Naperville Heritage Society.)

This poster advertises land sales in Illinois, "the Garden State of America." During the 1830s, Congress passed a series of laws establishing a federal land policy of preemption. Squatters living on the land could own up to 160 acres of surveyed government land for the low price of $1.25 per acre, with the understanding that they would either live on the land or commit to clearing and farming on the land for at least five years. The price per acre for choice real estate went up as government land was bought. (Courtesy of *Harper's Weekly*, June 6, 1863.)

Lisle, Illinois, shown in this vintage photograph, was settled by the Hatch brothers in 1832 just after the Black Hawk War and named after a town in New York. The area was originally inhabited by Potawatomi Indians for several hundred years, but with the advent of a few businesses such as a tavern, a general store, and a barbershop, it became quite a gathering place for residents. Dairy farms and brick making were its early industries. The locals voted in 1850 to create the Lisle township within DuPage County. The Chicago, Burlington & Quincy Railroad line opened in 1864 and carried passengers and freight from Aurora through the fledgling towns of Naperville, Lisle, Downers Grove, Hinsdale, and Berwyn to the west side of Chicago. The Lisle Depot made it much easier for dairy farmers to transport the milk to Chicago for sale and by 1912 was the largest milk shipping stop on the line.

Like many of the pioneers from the Northeast, Capt. Joseph Naper was born in Vermont. He was the son of Robert Naper and Sarah Hawley, married Alameda Landon in 1823, and raised seven children. A seafaring man, he had learned shipbuilding from his father but soon found out that he had another calling. He wanted to own land and farm. A courageous visionary, he pursued his passion, traveled westward to Ohio, and arrived in Chicago in 1831 with his family and friends. With the help of the Preemption Act of 1830, he purchased 180 acres of land by the West Branch of the DuPage River and laid out plans for its development. He demonstrated leadership and town planning skills, founded Naper's Settlement, and was elected first president of the Village of Naperville in 1857. He died in 1862 and is buried alongside his wife in the Naperville cemetery. (Above left and right, courtesy of Naperville Heritage Society; right, courtesy of Akshat Sahai.)

Now well known for its quiet, tree-lined streets; charming architecture; and thriving commercial district full of unique shops and restaurants, Naperville is a city that has been crowned with many awards. In 1839, after DuPage County was split from Cook County, Naperville became the county seat, which was held until 1868. Spanning over 39 square miles, Naperville, as of the 2021 census, has a population density of at least 3,800 people per square mile. With a population that includes 72 percent white, 19 percent Asian, 5 percent Hispanic or Latino, and 4 percent black, the area boasts a 10-mile technology corridor housing large corporations. Companies like Nokia, Nalco, British Petroleum, and Calamos Investments employ thousands of Naperville residents. Over the last decade, Naperville has been named "2nd Best Place to Live in the US," "One of the Nation's Safest Places to Live," and "the Best City in the US for Early Retirement." Nationally ranked North Central College, Edward Elmhurst Healthcare, and two large school districts contribute strongly to Naperville's high quality of life. (Courtesy of Akshat Sahai.)

Two

The Greene Family's "We Six"

Do whatever you do intensely.
The artist is the man who leaves the crowd and goes pioneering.
With him there is an idea which is his life.

—Robert Henri, *The Art Spirit*

The Greene family has a royal bloodline of French, English, German, and even Jewish heritage from centuries past. The family lineage can be traced from 1202 to 1635 in England and from 1635 to the present in America. The Greenes were descendants of Charlemagne, also known as Charles the Great, King of the Franks, and Emperor of the West. Lora La Mance's records from 1904 contain the earliest tracings of the Greene family genealogy and are later referenced by William Bertram Greene in his book *The Greenes on the East Branch of the DuPage*.

La Mance writes, "The beginning of the Greene family is shrouded in the night of the unchronicled story of centuries ago. A date or two comes down to us. The hazy figure of Lord Alexander rises like a ghost from his seven centuries of dust." He was a knight of the king's court, the great-great-grandson of Alen de la Zouche, the uncle of William the Conqueror, and the great-grandson of one of the Norman nobles who invaded England in 1066 with William the Conqueror. King John, then the ruler of both England and France, pleased with the loyalty and support from Lord Alexander during a rebellion that raged in England, granted the vast estate of Boketon in Northampton to him. Soon after, Lord Alexander assumed the surname of his chief estate, de Greene de Boketon, which translates to "Lord of the Park of the Deer Enclosure." The historian Halstead notes that the Greenes at one time were the largest land owners in all of England. Alexander de Greene de Boketon is the first Lord de Greene, and his estate with over 6,000 acres gave him the ranking of a baronage. He would be the foremost ancestor in the line of Greenes.

In 1215, King John of England was forced to sign the Magna Carta, which stated that the king was not above the law of the land and must protect the rights of the people. Lord Alexander was among the nobles who put their united protests in the hands of 25 lords who presented the Magna Carta to the king and forced him to sign the document. Today, the Magna Carta is considered one of the most important documents in the history of democracy. One of the signers was Roger, Earl of Winchester, whose great-great-granddaughter Lucie de la Zouche married the great-great-grandson of Sir Alexander de Greene, Lord Thomas Greene. Thus, the Greene family was a branch of the de la Zouche family; in fact, the historian Edward Gibbon stated that this family carried the strongest strain of royal blood in all of Europe.

John Greene of Rhode Island

Son of Robert Greene of
Bowbridge Hill, Dorsetshire, England.
Came to Boston, Mass., 1635

Commissioner for Warwick to Court of Commissioners of Rhode Island . . . 1651-1663
General Recorder . . . 1652-1654
Attorney General . . . 1657-1660
Assistant Attorney General 1660-73-77-78-80-89-90
Captain 1664-1683
Patentee named in Royal Charter . . 1662
Deputy for Warwick to General Assembly, R. I. 1664-74-75-77
Agent to England for Vindication of the Charter 1670
Major for the Main . 1683-86-90-1701-1706
Councillor of the Royal Province of New England . . . 1686-1689
Deputy Governor of R. I. . . 1690-1700

Several men by the name of Greene came to the colonies during the great Puritan migration into Massachusetts from 1630 to 1640, most of them settling in New England. Among them were two men, both named John Greene. Incidentally, both had wives named Joan. The similarity, however, ends here. John Greene of Quidnesset was born in 1606, sailed from England in 1635 on the ship *Matthew of London* to the British West Indies, and later settled in Quidnesset, Rhode Island. Interested in building and developing wilderness, he purchased 100 acres in Quidnesset in 1651 and established an Indian trading post with partner Richard Smith in the wilderness of the Narragansett Bay. He is believed to have died in 1695 in Rhode Island. This vintage flyer announces the arrival of the other John Greene to Rhode Island. Born in 1620, he sailed to New England in 1635 on the ship *James of London*. He spent most of his adult life in the public service of the colony and was the deputy governor of Rhode Island. He died in 1708 and was buried in Warwick, Rhode Island.

Royal blood from the kings of England, France, and Russia courses through the Greene family veins. Research conducted by Lora La Mance reveals that the 21st generation after Robert the Strong (duke in 861) was Robert of Gillingham, England, who had two sons named John Greene and Richard Greene. John Greene of Quidnesset was the direct descendant of John Greene, whereas John Greene of Warwick, Rhode Island, better known as "The Surgeon," was the great-great-grandfather of Nathanael Greene. Greene family members Kathy Streeton Issa (left) and Elizabeth "Betsy" Hibbard Greene (right) are paying homage to the sculpture of Nathanael Greene at the US Capitol Rotunda in Washington, DC. His leadership and brilliant campaign as a commander in the Continental army ended the British occupation of the South. History records Nathanael as the most trusted and dependable servant of Gen. George Washington in service of his country.

Family crests and coats of arms are powerful family symbols passed down through generations. They were commonly used throughout the 11th to 17th centuries and are meaningful reminders for families. The symbolism in the coat of arms characterizes the ancestors' achievements and status in society—a real testament to a family's legacy. Depicted is the colorful and decorative de Greene family coat of arms, a reminder of the royal ancestry of Lord Alexander de Greene de Boketon, which translates to "Lord of the Park of the Deer Enclosure." A green in ancient England was a park, and Boketon is an old word meaning "bucks" and "town," which later morphed into Boughton. The three bucks trippant on an azure field are appropriate symbols of the peaceful agricultural heritage of the Greene family. The Latin motto on the Greene coat of arms, *Nec timeo nec sperno*, means "I Neither Fear Nor Despise." The motto was originally a challenging war cry or slogan and served as a convenient identification in the battlefield for a fallen soldier wearing full armor.

Six generations after John Greene of Quidnesset, his descendant Daniel Moon Greene came to DuPage County in 1835 and settled by the East Branch of the DuPage River. Daniel Moon Greene was born in 1807 to Richard Greene and Lydia Latham, both from Wallingford, Vermont. He and his bride, Elizabeth Venelia Trowbridge, acquired three tracts of lovely dense rolling woodland from the government at $3 per acre. Their 250-acre farm was east of the river on either side of the present Route 53 between Seventy-First and Seventy-Fifth Streets, now known as Camp Greene Wood. Depicted is an anonymous sketch of their homestead named Nine Oaks, built around 1838, west of Route 53 on the oak-shaded sloping lawn. The charming old house burned to the ground in the early 1900s. (Courtesy of Mary Lou Wehrli.)

Pictured in 1884 are family members at Daniel Moon Greene's 50th wedding anniversary celebration. From left to right are (seated) Greene's spouse Elizabeth Venelia Trowbridge, Daniel Moon Greene, and daughter Caroline; (standing) daughter Hattie Grace, son Edward, and daughter Maria. Two of their offspring, Frances and Venelia, tragically died at younger ages. Elizabeth was the sister of the well-known author James T. Trowbridge, and her writing skills are well displayed in the sketch *A Journey to Illinois in 1835*, which was read at the golden wedding celebration. None of the Daniel Moon Greene descendants elected to stay on the farm, but successive generations kept in close contact. They became the "city cousins" of the Oak Cottage Greenes and were perceived as the link to the then sophisticated changing world.

This vintage photograph portrays William Briggs Greene with his wife, Harriet Meeker Greene. William Briggs was the grandson of Richard Greene of Wallingford, Vermont, a direct descendant of John Greene of Quidnesset. Following in the footsteps of his uncle Daniel Moon Greene, William Briggs came to Illinois in 1842. Only 23 at the time, he taught at the Goodrich School for several winters and worked on farms in the summers to secure funds to purchase land. In 1843, William Briggs bought 200 lovely, wooded acres of land at $5 an acre from the widow of the Goodrich family. Two years later, he returned to Vermont to fulfill another dream; he married Harriet Elizabeth Meeker, who came from a sheltered and cultured home and heroically adjusted to life on a farm in a log cabin surrounded by nine oak trees. They had six children, but only four remained—Laura, Helen, William Spencer, and Gertrude—after two were lost in early infancy. Despite all the challenges, a tough pioneering spirit prevailed, and the family never let their grief overpower their enthusiasm and respect for life. William Briggs and Harriet Meeker were known to be an extraordinarily handsome couple. Harriet Meeker had great personal beauty and was often described as very creative and an ardent lover of nature. William Spencer would say that his mother "would take nothing and make a present out of it."

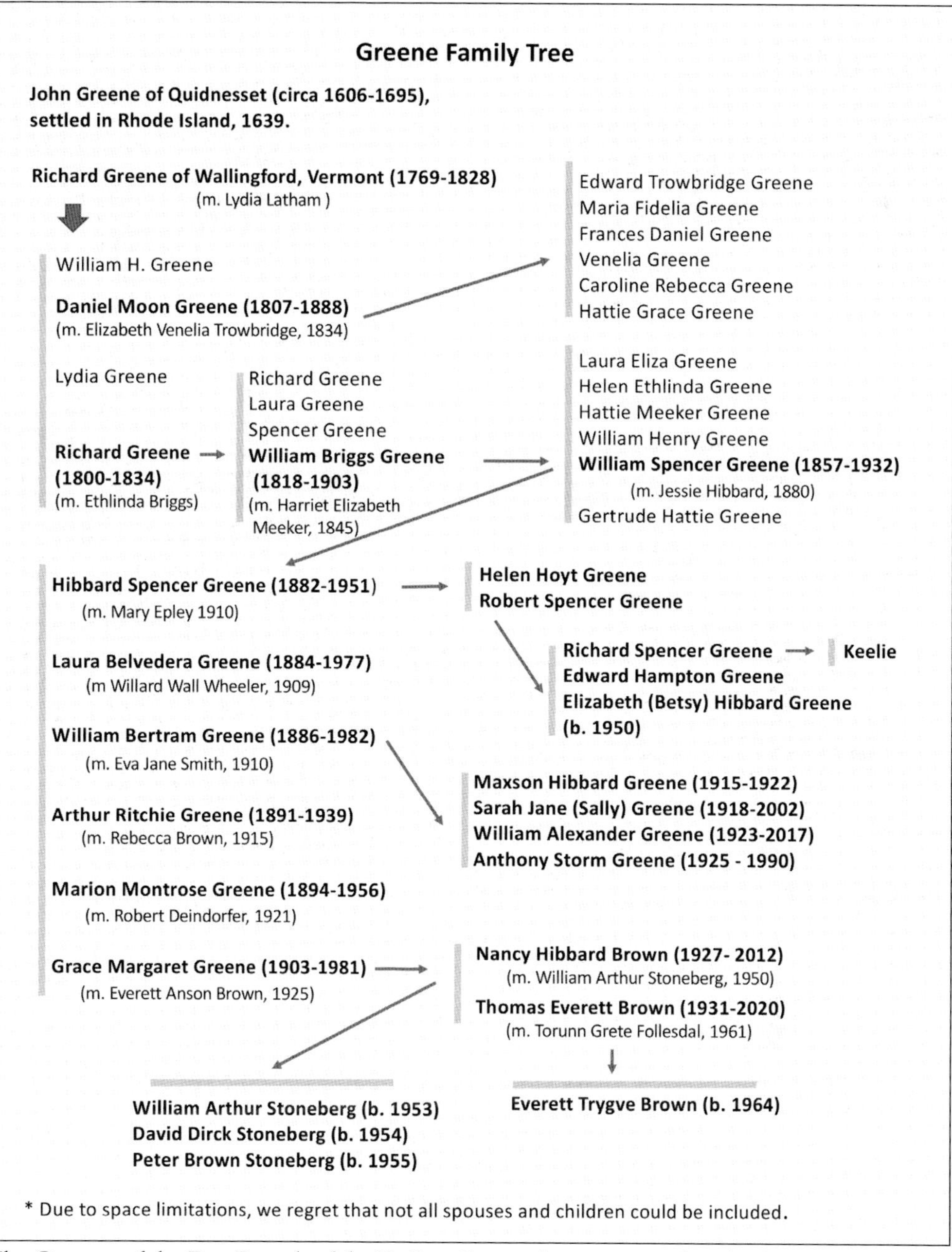

The Greenes of the East Branch of the DuPage River who are covered in this book are portrayed in this family tree. As noted, not all spouses or children could be included due to space limitations. Three generations, starting with William Spencer Greene, grew up, lived, and laughed in the Greene family homestead, which included Oak Cottage and the family barn on the bur oak–studded grounds. Six generations actually lived at Oak Cottage, whereas seven generations visited or were fortunate to experience life at Oak Cottage, from Daniel Moon to Keelie Veruschka Greene, the great-grand-daughter of Hibbard Spencer Greene. Richard Spencer Greene; his wife, Cindy; and daughter Keelie were caretakers of Oak Cottage for one year in 1982–1983 and were the last residents of the family home.

Portrayed above is a unique and creative painting of the Greene family homestead, as seen from the south, by Thomas Everett Brown, the last person to have been born in Oak Cottage. Additionally, an aerial perspective of the Oak Cottage and the barn at the corner of Hobson and Greene Roads in Naperville is shown below. William Spencer Greene used local timber and quarried limestone to build the largest barn in DuPage County, with 14,000 square feet of shelter for animals and crops. Wood for the stoves and fireplace were chopped by hand, and produce was raised in gardens and orchards. The dairy farm prospered. Corn, oats, alfalfa hay, and wheat grew readily in the glacial black soil of Illinois and were mostly harvested by hand. Oxen and horses were kept for work and transportation; pigs, sheep, chickens, and cows were raised to provide food. Bees were kept for their honey.

This photograph of the charming Greene family home affectionately known as Oak Cottage dates back to the early summer of 1891. In 1850, after living in the log cabin for five years, William Briggs Greene built the main section of Oak Cottage to make room for his growing family. The log cabin, just in front of Oak Cottage, was not saved for posterity. Those were simple yet happy days. The important values of laughter, gaiety, wit, and humor were cultivated along with a deep respect for all that nature had to offer. Soaking in the sun after a harsh winter, William Briggs Greene and Harriet Meeker Greene are on the lawn along with siblings Laura and William, seated on the porch are William Spencer and Jessie Hibbard, and Hibbard Spencer Greene is on the pony (Dexter).

This artwork looked down upon six generations of the Greene family for over a century. Gifts of nature such as leaves, grains, and grasses were placed creatively to bestow blessings on both family members and visiting guests to Oak Cottage. The blessings bestowed were always full of love and emphasized family unity. The artist was none other than Harriet Meeker Greene, the first mistress of Oak Cottage, who had a robust enthusiasm for life and a keen appreciation of the beauty of nature. The framed artwork hung in the living room of the Oak Cottage for as long as family members lived there. It is now a part of the family treasures that have been placed with Naperville Heritage Society.

Pictured above around 1904 is a quaint collection of the "We Six" clan, children of William Spencer Greene. From left to right are Hibbard Spencer Greene, Laura Belvedera Greene, Arthur

This monument at the paddleboat quarry at Riverwalk Park in Naperville is dedicated to the farm families who pioneered the Naperville community. A style of the steel plow developed by John Deere in 1837 highlights the hard work and perseverance of the early settlers in their efforts to cultivate the prairie for crops and pasture. (Courtesy of Akshat Sahai.)

Ritchie Greene, Grace Margaret Greene, William Bertram Greene, and Marion Montrose Greene.

Details of the monument shown on previous page are seen here. The third line proclaims: "W.S. GREENE FARM." William Spencer Greene was the second-born son to William Briggs Greene and Harriet Meeker Greene after 12 years of their marriage. As the only surviving son, he took over management of the farm from his father and instituted many progressive ideas, such as the building of a handsome new red barn and the replacement of sheep with cows. The thriving dairy business that he started was robust even after 100 years. (Courtesy of Akshat Sahai.)

St. John's Episcopal Church in downtown Naperville, Illinois, was built and consecrated in 1865. The land on the corner of Jefferson Avenue and Ellsworth Street was donated by Morris Sleight, a real estate developer. The Greenes joined other families to build this spiritual home, which served a growing congregation for over 100 years. The church grew to over 350 members in the 1870s. As the family gathered for baptisms, confirmations, weddings, and funerals, St. John's became an integral part of the Greenes' lives. The last service as a church was the memorial service for Everett Anson Brown, husband of Grace Greene Brown, in 1968.

Members of the Greene family, Tom Brown, Betsy Greene, Everett Trygve Brown and Faye, Tom's third wife, reminisce outside the relocated St. John's Episcopal Church in Naperville. Threatened with demolition in 1969, community members, led by Jane Sindt, a local activist, banded together to save the church. Through fundraising efforts, the beautiful Carpenter Gothic church was relocated (in three parts) to the city museum site in 1970. Renamed Century Memorial Chapel, it became the nucleus of today's 13-acre Naper Settlement. The Naperville Heritage Society was started in 1969 and was instrumental in the creation of Naper Settlement. Nancy Hibbard Brown, daughter of Grace Greene Brown, helped to found the Naperville Heritage Society. She and other champions generated a fresh commitment to local heritage.

Portrayed in Sunday-best attire are Jessie Hibbard and William Spencer Greene. William Spencer Greene was born to William Briggs Greene and Harriet Meeker Greene in 1857. He wed Jessie Hibbard in 1880, and the rest was history. William Spencer would often speak of his young bride, who weighed less than 100 pounds and had a tiny waist, a mark of distinction in those days. They were the proud parents of the "We Six" generation.

William Spencer and Jessie Greene (seated) pose with their six children in 1930 in front of Oak Cottage. Three boys and three girls were born to them over a span of 21 years. The dairy farm that William Spencer started was so successful that it provided enough income to send all six of his children to college. Loyalty, courage, integrity, and honesty were at the core of his character and made him a source of strength for Jessie and their children.

At left, in 1905, the "We Six" clan pose on a fence by Oak Cottage. From left to right are Hibbard Spencer Greene, Laura Belvedera Greene, William Bertram Greene, Arthur Ritchie Greene, Marion Montrose Greene, and Grace Margaret Greene. Most photographs in the early 1900s were planned; folks dressed up for the occasion and were creative about their settings. Below, in an image apparently taken on the same day, they chose to stand in a line with a backdrop of the verdant nature around Oak Cottage.

Shown are Hibbard Spencer Greene; his wife, Mary Epley, and their grandchildren, from left to right, John Ross, Edward "Tad" Greene, and Betsy Greene. Hibbard, the first of the "We Six" clan, could not have been better cast for his role as big brother. Conscientious, ambitious, and responsible, he was a born leader. He was the first to make the half-mile walk to the Goodrich School. In 1910, he married Mary Epley, a woman with a rich artistic background who added much flair to the growing Greene family. He gave freely of his time and talents for various causes. The harmony of the "We Six" clan was indeed fostered by Hibbard's ideals, for he made sure that they were a congenial group, which ultimately grew into a mutual admiration society. His impressive funeral service was held in 1951 at St. Paul's Episcopal Church in Milwaukee.

MY FAMILY
Laura Greene Wheeler

What is it that makes a closely-knit family?
It is more than love, more than congeniality,
It is a quality, taught or ingrained, which
puts the needs of others first – one for all, all for one.

Long ago at Oak Cottage our grandparents
operated on that plane and through the years it
has become more and more ingrained, a pattern.

My earliest memories are of the love and
harmony of our three-generation family where
parents and grandparents were an example to my
five brothers and sisters and me. We don't just love –
we like each one and have greater happiness and
fun with each other, without misunderstanding
or boredom, than could be so with others.

The Greenes waxed poetic to express their love for one another and to celebrate birthdays, weddings, graduations, and other family events. This doggerel was written by Laura Wheeler expressing the strong bond that held the Greene family together, and her words ring true even today. Laura Greene Wheeler was the second of the "We Six" clan. Born in 1884, she married Willard Wheeler in 1909. She was a radiant and inspiring person, a veritable mother to all. As the first daughter, she became her mother's helper, and her Grandfather Greene called her the "Little Peacemaker." In later years, she was the glue that held the extended family together, even after moving to California. She was a witty, wise, and sensitive reporter of the doings of the Greene family for 70–80 years. She gave generously of herself and was a comforter not only to her family but to friends as well. She often said her days "were never long enough." She died in 1977 at the age of 93, and her family keenly felt her loss.

Pictured from left to right are William Bertram Greene, Hibbard Spencer Greene, and Laura Belvedera Greene. Laura was born two years after Hibbard in 1884 and was a pink-cheeked bouncing baby, according to her mother, Jessie. William Bertram, the second son born to William Spencer and Jessie Hibbard, was the namesake of his father and grandfather Greene.

Arthur Ritchie Greene, the fourth of the "We Six" clan, was a welcome baby at Oak Cottage. He was a very handsome child and delighted his siblings with his pranks and high spirits. He loved horses and was very diligent in taking care of them. Arthur took over the management of the farm in 1914 and continued to manage it for over 20 years. His unfailing honesty, charm, and humor and his love of people brought him many friends from across the community.

Arthur Ritchie Greene was competent professionally and instituted many modern improvements on the farm. He built the round concrete silos, procured tractors and milking machines, and was quick to adopt hybrid corn and other advances in seeds. He married Rebecca Brown in 1915, but he was soon troubled by broken hopes, a broken marriage, and ill health. He died in 1939 at the young age of 48, the first break in the congenial circle of the "We Six," which brought deep sadness within the family.

A most precious keepsake, this photograph from early 1916 was taken under a bur oak tree on the lawns surrounding Oak Cottage. Identifiable persons are William Spencer Greene and his wife, Jessie Hibbard, seated in the center. Maxson, son of William Bertram Greene, is on his grandmother's lap. Sitting between the grandparents is little Helen Hoyt Greene, and sitting on the grass is her brother Robert Spencer Greene. Standing from left to right are an unidentified woman, Grace in her early teens, Mary Epley and Hibbard Spencer Greene, Jane and William Bertram Greene, Marion (nine years senior to Grace), and an unidentified couple.

This photograph, taken in 1955, shows the three daughters of William Spencer and Jessie Hibbard Greene, who were known as the beloved "Three Graces." Pictured from left to right, Laura Belvedera, Marion Montrose, and Grace Margaret were pioneer matriarchs. Not only were they gracious and kind, but they were also hardworking and had the qualities of character and wisdom that were needed to negotiate a hard life on the prairie. William Bertram Greene referred to them as "My Valentines" in poetic fervor in 1943: "Beauty, rare and Disposition / Loving, sweet and saccharine / All admire Hearts afire / our triple Valentines."

This photograph of Jessie Hibbard was taken in 1931 shortly before her passing. She is shown holding and admiring her granddaughter Nancy, daughter of Grace Greene Brown. The grandchildren knew her as Mimi. Jessie had a personality that was warm and glowing. Her endless patience, gentle persuasion, and strong sense of duty and responsibility inspired the children and became a legacy to her grandchildren. Inspiring and encouraging her during her life was this quote by Phillips Brooks found among her papers: "Character is like bells which ring out sweet music, and which when touched, accidentally even, resound with sweet music."

Leave it to kids to find simple pleasures and joys in everyday farm equipment. Here, Greene family cousins, great-grandchildren of William Spencer Greene and Jessie Hibbard, are exploring a parked milk delivery truck in front of the Greene barn. From left to right are Kathy Streeton (grandchild of Laura Greene and Willard Wheeler), Mason Ross, John Ross, and Richard Greene (grandchildren of Hibbard Spencer Greene). In the early 1900s, farmers welcomed the shift from animal to mechanically powered implements, innovations that would relieve them from backbreaking and time-consuming hard labor while raising farm efficiency and production. Implements used in the past, such as the old ox yoke, the grain cradle, and horse-drawn buggies, became treasured farm relics. The Greene cousins were the first to experience and be intrigued by this transition from animal-driven implements to the more modern engine-driven tractors and trucks.

Here, Grace and Marion are enjoying a moment of merriment. Holding an axe in her hand, Marion pretends to behead Grace, whose head is on a pedestal purportedly used for preparing chickens and other animals for dinner.

Grace (left) and her sister Marion are playing jacks on the concrete stoop in front of the cottage. Jacks is one of the oldest games on the planet, played across the globe in many cultures with small variations. The simplest throw consists of tossing up one stone, the jack, and picking up one or more jacks from the table while it is in the air. This continues until all five stones have been picked up.

William Spencer Greene and his wife of 50 years, Jessie Hibbard Greene (seated center), celebrated this special anniversary in 1930 with a grand open house for over 100 guests from Chicago, Aurora, and the surrounding neighborhood. They were married on September 29, 1880, at the Church of the Ascension, Chicago by the late Rev. Arthur Ritchie. Among other guests were all of their six children (the "We Six" as they are fondly called), William Bertram Greene, Marion Montrose Deindorfer, Laura Belvedera Wheeler, Grace Margaret Brown, Arthur Ritchie Greene, and Hibbard Spencer Greene. Hibbard Spencer, who had been abroad for the preceding seven years, returned to America for the occasion. Seated on the grass are, from left to right, grandchildren Jack Deindorfer, Bob Deindorfer, Alex Greene, Sarah "Sally" Jane Greene, Bob Spencer Greene, Tony Storm Greene, and Nancy Hibbard Brown.

Grace Margaret Greene and her mother, Jessie Hibbard Greene, are sitting in a beam of sunshine outside Oak Cottage, the grounds partially shaded by the large oak trees. The vivid personality and tomboyish behavior of Grace gave the family endless delight and entertainment. She got away with many of the rights and privileges that her older brothers and sisters had been denied. Her plaintive and charming "But Papa, times have changed!" tugged at her father's heartstrings, and he would gladly give in.

Early life on the farm and having parents with strong traditional values had set the stage for Grace Margaret Greene's success. She always found time to come back to the farm and help her brother Arthur, 12 years her senior, with mowing and binding the hay. Grace would drive the tractor, and Arthur would operate the binder. Early binders were horse drawn, and later models were tractor drawn. Both would eventually be replaced by the combine harvester, which combined reaping, threshing, gathering, and winnowing into a single process.

Grace Margaret Greene was the last of the "We Six," born in 1903. She attended Goodrich School, followed by high school in Naperville, and then the University of Illinois. At college, she was a member of Pi Beta Phi and was elected a beauty queen. Grace excelled in her studies and had many friends. Her vivid personality, tomboy behavior, and sweet smile won her popularity and many friends. After college, she continued the family tradition by teaching at a county school. Airplanes were a novelty at the time, and many of her beaux were pilots who would lavish her with gifts, sometimes even by parachute. She chose Everett Anson Brown, the brother of Arthur's wife, who had been a frequent visitor and was familiar with the traditions at the Greene family home. Grace married Everett in St. John's Episcopal Church in 1925. Together, they became the heart of the beloved Oak Cottage.

Basking in dappled sunshine under the bur oak trees surrounding Oak Cottage with their mother Grace are Nancy Hibbard Brown and Thomas Everett Brown, born at Oak Cottage in 1927 and 1931, respectively. Just as an acorn becomes an oak tree, generations of Greenes have been nurtured by Oak Cottage and its surroundings. Most of these mighty bur oaks, a symbol of life, strength, survival, hope, and encouragement, have perished. However, right across from Oak Cottage, hundreds of acorns from the famous Hobson oak were gathered in 2016, germinated by Morton Arboretum, and found loving new landscapes.

The proud mother stands with her son Thomas Everett Brown at his graduation from the University of Illinois in 1954 with an architecture degree. After graduation, Brown served as a US Air Force jet pilot, enjoying a government sponsored, three-year tour of all corners of scenic Texas. In 1958, he began an erratic odyssey, which included travel in Europe, a year working in Sweden, some time back at the farm designing houses in Naperville, a job in Australia, and finally settling in San Francisco in 1960.

Nancy and Thomas Brown were the third generation to know the fun of growing up on the farm at Oak Cottage. Brother and sister are in a horse-driven wagon harvesting apples from the large orchard south of the barn. The orchard had varieties for early summer, August sweets, Snow apples, and good winter apples. Apples were mostly eaten raw and between meals year-round. One year, the winter crop yielded 13 barrels of apples, which were stored in the cool cellar under the central portion of Oak Cottage.

Everett Anson Brown and his wife, Grace, are enjoying a lazy afternoon on the south porch of Oak Cottage while their children are busy at work harvesting apples. Grace, the youngest of the "We Six," was raised not only by her parents but also by five siblings. She was the radiant and energetic mistress of Oak Cottage for 50 years (1931–1981), longer than either of her predecessors, Harriet and Jessie. The wholesome country living and the frequent large gatherings of the clan that Everett and Grace hosted were important parts of their heritage.

Nancy Hibbard Brown was 23 years old when she married William Arthur Stoneberg in 1950. Nancy lived in Naperville with her family, close to Oak Cottage for several years, and looked after her mother, Grace, during her final years. Nancy and Bill moved to Florida in November 1982, after attending the grand family reunion at Oak Cottage a few months earlier. Later, they joined two of their sons who had settled in Northern California.

This photograph, taken in 1958, shows Nancy with her husband, William Arthur Stoneberg, and their three boys riding in a 1915 Model T outside Oak Cottage. Nancy's children were born roughly a year apart; William Arthur Stoneberg was born in 1953, David Dirck Stoneberg in 1954, and Peter Brown Stoneberg in 1955. They were to know Oak Cottage and the farm intimately, riding the last horse (Bluebell), riding the tractor mower with their Grandpa Brown, and seeing the final farm auction of the dairy herd in 1964. Years later, Daniel Peter Stoneberg, born July 1981 to Peter and Christine Stoneberg, would make his first visit to his great-grandmother Grace in August 1981, when he was about two weeks old.

Thomas Brown's Ford Model T club gathers at the family farm in 1952. For his entire life, Brown had loved automobiles and airplanes. This followed the paradigm shift from covered wagons and horse-drawn sleighs to mechanical engines in the previous generation. The Ford Model T was an iconic automobile and dominated sales from 1908 to the early 1920s. Brown had a fascination for these early cars and even helped start the aforementioned club, where he would show off his own 1915 model that he would keep for virtually the rest of his life.

Tom Brown had a remarkable energy and passion for life, to explore the unknown and new, as did his pioneer forefathers. He was a trained pilot and served in the US Air Force in the 1950s. Here, he is shown in uniform aboard his plane.

Tom Brown married Torunn Grete Follesdal, a Norwegian architect, in Oslo, Norway, on November 22, 1961. They returned to San Francisco to work and to continue schooling at Berkeley, where both studied during the turbulent years of the late 1960s. Tom's respect for old-world tradition and values and his nostalgia for the farm life that he had experienced while growing up at Oak Cottage never left him. In spite of his travels and moving to California, he held onto hundreds of old photographs and many artifacts from the homestead, including farm relics and Oak Cottage furniture. Indeed, he experienced the world and life through a larger lens than most.

Everett Trygve Brown was born in San Francisco in 1964. He grew up in California but spent many summers and Christmases with his grandmother Grace and is one of the last progenies to have stayed in Oak Cottage. He cherishes many childhood memories of time spent at Oak Cottage like summers playing in the sandbox or being pulled on a sled through the snowy landscape in the winters.

Posing together at a photograph studio in Chicago, Illinois, around 1971 are seven-year-old Trygve Brown, sporting a bowler hat, and his parents, Tom and Torunn, also decked in period hats and clothing.

This 1984 photograph portrays, from left to right, Trygve Brown, Anne (Tom Brown's second wife), and Trygve's father, Tom, by their favorite automobile, a 1915 Ford Model T. The trio drove the car from the family barn in Naperville, where it had stayed for 34 years, to their California home, a 19-day odyssey at 35 miles per hour with a "California or bust" sign on the back! Tom had owned this car from 1950 and finally sold it to his nephew Peter Stoneberg for the same price he paid for it—$60. Tom loved old planes as well as old cars. Here, he is proudly standing with his son just before they flew his 1942 Stearman biplane from California to Wisconsin in 1990.

As is evident from the above photographs, Tom Brown sported the same carefree cuteness he had as a baby well into his senior years, with the wisdom of maintaining a positive well-being and kindness in the face of physical decline as he aged. Brown had an illustrious career as an architect, establishing his own firm in San Francisco in 1970, which he ran until 2000. He even designed a downtown plan for his hometown of Naperville in the 1970s in which he envisioned a tranquil and beautiful walkway along the DuPage River. The plan materialized in 1981, and the Riverwalk, featuring 1.75 miles of brick paths, fountains, bridges, and outdoor sculptures, is now considered the "Crown Jewel of Naperville."

One wonders what sentiments may have contributed to the making of this scale model of Oak Cottage by Tom Brown as a child. The last of the Greenes to be born there, he was witness to the transformation from old-world farming to technology-driven tractors. The homes that the early settlers built were modest and typically consisted of two rectangles in the shape of an L, with a living room, a bedroom, and a kitchen in the wing off the larger rectangle. A narrow staircase would lead to a few bedrooms, conforming to the space below and the angles of the roof above.

Not only did Thomas Everett Brown have the creative freedom and the resources to pursue his passions, but his gentle hands on the hitching post also speak of the fond emotions associated with this Oak Cottage relic.

Leveraging his passions for both art and architecture, Thomas Everett Brown was an avid painter. His painting of a snow-wrapped Oak Cottage in the winter with a horse-driven sleigh is reminiscent of a Currier & Ives winter scenery lithograph from the late 1800s.

This photograph was taken at an annual school picnic. The "We Six" clan attended the Goodrich School, where their grandfather William Briggs had taught. In 1858, the school had eight grades, was a half-mile walk from Oak Cottage, and served the children of the early settlers. Grace learned the three Rs at the school, as had her siblings. The present school, Goodrich Elementary, built in the 1920s, is in the community of Woodridge, Illinois, on the corner of Hobson Road and Route 53.

Young Tom Brown, a coeditor of the Goodrich school newspaper, wrote this poem:

THE SNOW MAN

I'm a jolly snowman,
Very big and fat
I've a nice round face,
and a funny old hat
Two coals for my eyes
And a stick for my nose,
And a good warm heart
(though that never shows.)
But being very fat
doesn't bother me.
I'll stand in the sun
and soon I'll be
As thin as thin
as the poplar tree.

Outside activities were limitless for the neighborhood families and their children. Winter did not deter this group from sharing a moment on the fence facing the setting sun by the barn. Long wool skirts and jackets with wool hats helped keep them warm in the nippy air. In William Bertram Greene's own words from 1963, "We worked so hard, we had so little, and we had such a rich and happy childhood! We had no great adventures, no high drama—just a good life."

Both William Spencer and his wife put great emphasis on social interactions with friends and neighbors and encouraged their children to have enough company to make up for any farm isolation. Neighbors often got together and entertained each other with indoor games such as charades or singing with piano accompaniment. Snow brought other fun opportunities. Families warmly dressed for the cold winter weather would huddle onto a sleigh pulled by a team of horses and ride through the snow crusted roads.

Three

Life at Oak Cottage

When held by the same family for a considerable period of time, the cottage may also come to represent the family, to become "the home, the gathering place," to which the far-flung family returns to renew contacts and once again experience the fundamental satisfactions of being a family.

—Greg Halseth

The word *cottage* evokes memories of a cozy dwelling surrounded by large oak trees, nestled on a hilltop by a meandering river and surrounded by rolling prairie grass. The sprawling farmhouse built by early settlers near the East Branch of the DuPage River in Naperville, Illinois, is just that. Built in 1850 and lovingly called Oak Cottage, the New England Colonial-style home provided a much-loved and much-lived-in place for six generations of the Greene family. Wings were added to the original farmhouse to accommodate the growing families. One senses that a deep, enduring pride has prompted the Greene family to regard the old homestead as a shrine. Life at Oak Cottage carried a sense of security, and family members could always *go back home.*

The spirit of Oak Cottage has been maintained according to the old traditions of community, of family kinship, of kindness and caring, and of being good neighbors. Those were unique times. Oak Cottage was a haven for many, and the Greene family children were encouraged to maintain an open house almost continually. Thoughtful parenting, living with due regard to age-old wisdoms and traditions, and having the will to welcome new age thinking all worked together to increase family bonds and nurture family relationships. The cultural heritage of putting the needs of others first has continued to inspire the expanding Greene family.

Oak Cottage continues to cast a spell of its own and has been home to more than 16 people living there at a time. "The simple home of a simple family, who met their joys with simple faith and steadfast hearts, it weaves its spell over all who enter its doors," wrote Laura Greene Wheeler, daughter of William Spencer Greene, back in 1962.

This view of Oak Cottage shows the two-story central portion built in 1850 by William Briggs Greene and Harriet Meeker Greene. At left, the east wing with its screened porches afforded pleasant summer living. The *L*-shaped west wing is obscured in this photograph. Later, one-story wings were added to accommodate their growing family, which included three of their six children who survived infancy: Laura, William Spencer, and Gertrude Greene. When William Spencer Greene assumed the management of the farm after his marriage to Jessie Hibbard in 1880, the

east wing was extended to give the senior Greenes a separate suite. Although more rooms were added to the west wing, the farmhouse was taxed to accommodate the two families, including William Spencer's six children and the necessary hired hands. The William Spencer Greene family lived for two more decades in this home. In 1928, Grace Greene Brown; her husband, Everett Anson Brown; and their two children, Nancy and Tom, moved from Downers Grove back to Oak Cottage.

This is a plaque from the Naperville Heritage Society installed by the front door of Oak Cottage. The society's plaque program fosters awareness, appreciation, and preservation of landmarks that are of architectural and historical importance to Naperville, Illinois. The plow logo depicted on the plaque is typical of the essential implement used in the 1800s by farmers to break and reshape the prairie. Also recognized on this plaque is William Briggs Greene, who built Oak Cottage in 1850. (Courtesy of Mary Lou Wehrli.)

The dining room at Oak Cottage was the scene of countless Greene family gatherings. The centerpiece shown on the table is now a family relic. Parents and grandparents encouraged the young ones to share stories of incidents at school, church, or on the playground with the group. Table etiquette was also engrained, such as do not spread your elbows; do not take big bites; do not make eating noises; do not ask for second helpings, wait to be asked; and ask to be excused to leave the table.

A white marble fireplace, framed family portraits, and braided rugs in the living room are restful and welcoming. The artful *God Bless Our Home* created by Harriet Meeker Greene around 1850 hangs over the doorway leading to the east wing of the house.

William Briggs Greene and Harriet Meeker Greene, parents of William Spencer Greene, chose marble from their native Vermont for the fireplace in 1850. Grace basks! In the 1880s, the Danby quarry, tucked a mile and a half underground inside Dorset mountain in Vermont, produced marble that was one of a kind and unparalleled, a clean white stone with overall veining.

Framed family photographs hanging on the walls, a beautiful mahogany highboy, a spindle wood bed, an old spinning wheel, and braided rugs complete the cozy cottage's master bedroom. This was the bedroom shared by Everett Anson Brown and Grace Greene Brown. One doorway leads to the bathroom, which separates the Browns' bedroom from the one beyond.

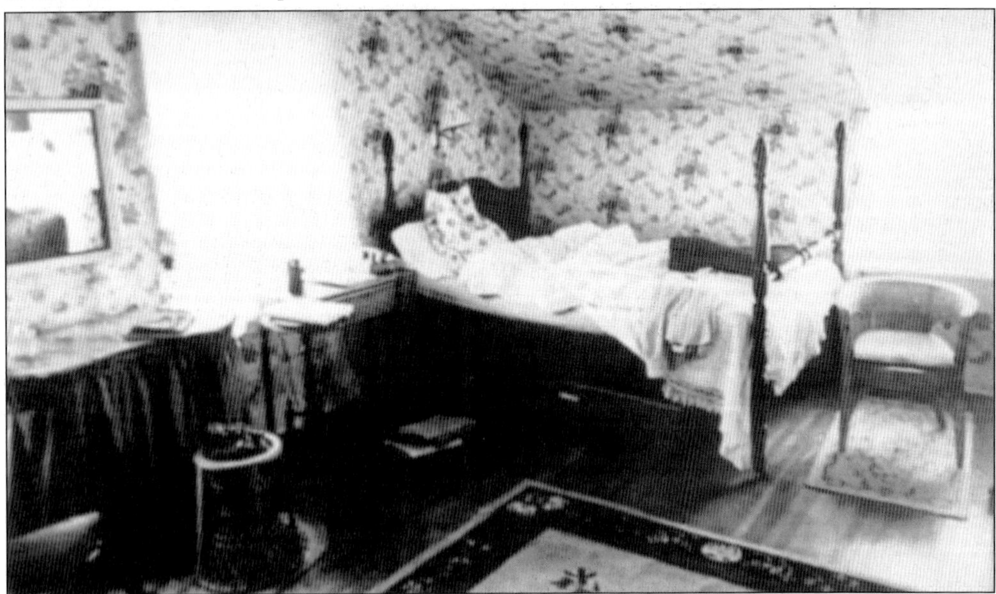

The upstairs rooms are tucked under the gable roof of the central portion of the home. While the grandparents of the "We Six" were alive, the children occupied the two smaller bedrooms upstairs, although they often had to share their bedrooms with guests such as the visiting minister. It was, at times, almost likened to a country hotel with hundreds of guests over the years. Each bedroom was equipped with a washstand, washbowl, soap dish, water pitcher, and chamber pot. Accoutrements for a guest were more ornate and even included a toothbrush.

This is a second kitchen and breakfast room. There is a wood-burning stove built up on bricks. A braided area rug and a cozy rocking chair add to the simple elegance of this sunny room. At one time, it was used as a living and dining room for the hired help. The three hired men, the cook, and a helper occupied adjoining rooms in the southwest corner of Oak Cottage.

This sketch of the second kitchen was the idea behind a remodeling. In 1951, while Grace Greene Brown and Everett Anson Brown were in California, Tom, their son and an architecture student, remodeled the back kitchen as a surprise gift. Of note is the wood-burning stove used by pioneers to bake or cook food, which was regulated by burning the correct amount of wood to get the right temperature.

An old sign right outside Oak Cottage advertises the family's dairy farm. The sign was nailed onto one of the bur oak trees that graced the lawn. Chicago offered a stable market for milk, and the Oak Cottage Dairy Farm was suitably located for this purpose. The milking parlor in the south wing of the barn housed up to 90 cows. Milk stored in heavy 75-pound cans was delivered to the Lisle Depot station, one of the original stops from Aurora to Chicago. The main purpose of the line at the time was to transport locally produced agricultural food products to the growing city of Chicago.

In this photograph, taken around 1905, the Greenes and their house guests take a milk wagon ride on a balmy summer evening. Music and witty conversations made it fun, moonlight was a bonus. Three could ride up on the driver's seat, and long plank seats could be laid along the length of the wagon. These wagons were the same ones used to transport milk and posed quite a challenge on the snow-covered rugged roads during winter months.

Grace Greene Brown is sitting in the heirloom rocker in her parlor, looking fondly at an album of family pictures. Over the Chickering piano is a large photograph of her mother, Jessie Hibbard Greene. The huge secretary at right displays the impressive collection of Indian arrowheads found on the family's 320-acre farm. On the floor is a braided rug, prevalent in many homes at the time and similar to many that were used throughout Oak Cottage.

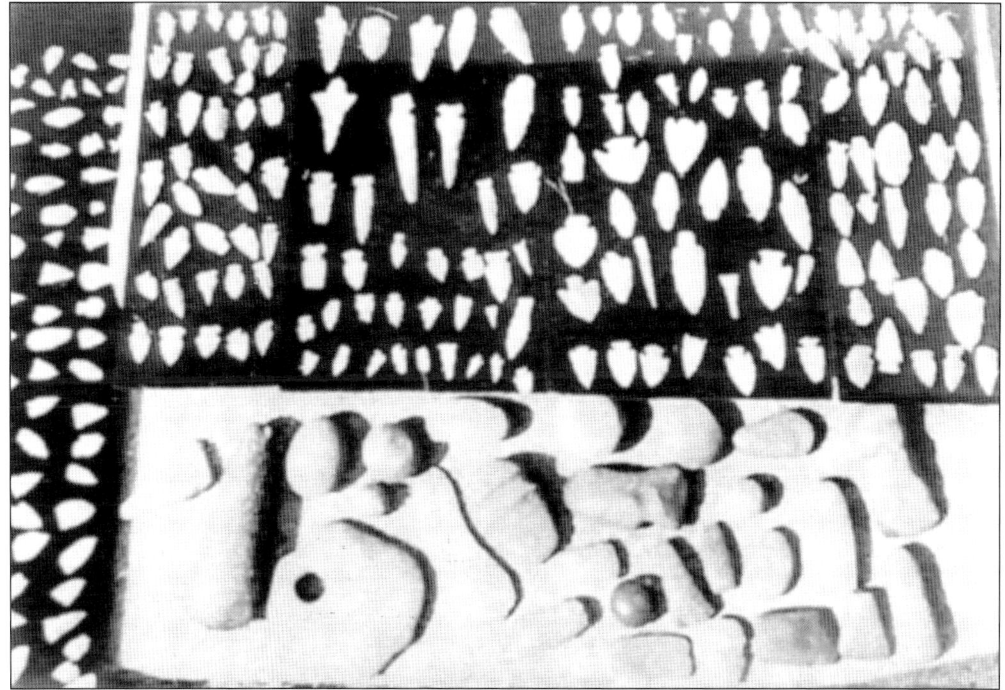

Displayed are the arrowheads found on and around the Greene family homestead. Numerous arrowheads were found by local farmers plowing their fields. William Spencer Greene was known to be an avid collector of these relics. His hired hands and farmers from nearby areas would bring them to him, and he would pay them for each one. With a substantial number of arrowheads and stone axes, his collection was donated to the Naperville Heritage Society.

Pictured is a Christmas gathering at Oak Cottage in 1940 with family and friends. From left to right are (first row) William Bertram Greene, Marion, Grace Greene Brown, her son Thomas Everett Brown, wearing a spiffy hat and holding the Merry Christmas greeting. Nancy Hibbard Brown, the daughter of Grace, is on the third row, second from right, with the bow in her hair. The rest are unidentified.

This was a Christmas greeting card from the Brown family. The card features the scale model of Oak Cottage that Tom Brown had created.

The Model T Ford parked outside the cottage is a tell-tale sign of the innovations in transportation during the early 1900s. At the time of this photograph, the Model T had become a relic, a thing of the past, not unlike Oak Cottage in the background. The combined harvester-thresher along with the corn picker, the milking machine, and the tractor that used gasoline for fuel had revolutionized the traditional farm operations. The old reaper was now a relic and stored in the woodshed.

Helen Hoyt Greene (left), daughter of Hibbard Spencer Greene, poses with her aunts, Marion Montrose Greene (center) and Grace Greene Brown (right), by the hitching post, which was used to tether horses to prevent them from straying. The hitching post became another relic as horse-drawn sleighs and wagons were soon replaced by motor vehicles with four wheels and an internal combustion engine.

The art of engraving on copper or steel started around the middle of the 15th century, but after the 1830s, most of the engravings were done in steel or steel-faced copper. The engravings have an almost silvery feel, and such engravings, like *The Village Blacksmith* shown at left, were treasured in many homes.

The last of the Greene family to have spent much of their lives at Oak Cottage are, from left to right, Nancy Hibbard Brown, Everett Anson Brown, Grace Greene Brown, and Thomas Everett Brown. Hanging on the wall above the sofa is the engraving of *The Village Blacksmith*, flanked on either side by portraits of William Spencer Greene and Jessie Hibbard Greene. Grace and her brother William Bertram Greene (who was 17 years older) were the last ones to call Oak Cottage home. They lived together and looked after one another in their final years. Thomas had moved to California, and Nancy lived in the neighborhood. Grace passed away in 1981, and the farmhouse passed to Forest Preserve District of DuPage County ownership. This marked the end of an era for the Greene homestead, concurrent with the end of farming as a vital force in DuPage County. Oak Cottage had been a witness to the ebb and flow of life for over 130 years: love, relationships, births, deaths, weddings, anniversaries, celebrations, seasonal transitions, and aging oak trees. It is now silent.

Four

The Greene Family Patriarch

Support good leaders, or be one yourself.

—William Bertram Greene

This is the story of William Bertram Greene (W.B. Greene), probably the Greene family's most notable personality, who was fondly known to most of the family as "Uncle Billy." He was the third of the "We Six" generation and was born in 1886 on September 4 at Oak Cottage. Tradition would have it that he be named William Briggs Greene after his grandfather. The discrepancy in "Bertram" rather than "Briggs" arose from the fact that they had a distant neighbor named William Briggs, who was rather unpleasant. Young Bill's parents felt impelled to pick another name while maintaining the WBG initials and chose Bertram as his middle name.

W.B. Greene conducted his life such that he would be of benefit to mankind. He was born more than a century ago, but the caliber of his thinking deserves immense respect and praise. He was a visionary who kept looking forward into the future and was ahead of his time. He was also a philanthropist and a businessman who supported causes that were not so popular in his time, such as the environment, the Girl Scouts, and the creation of pension plans for his employees. Above all, he served and protected his family through hardship, prejudice, failure, and, sometimes, total life catastrophe. His imagination, generosity, and business acumen benefited both his family and the public in great measure.

Traditions provide families with a sense of identity and belonging, a sense of continuity that transfers the family's values, history, and culture from one generation to the next. W.B. Greene was very aware of this and lived his life nurturing not only his dreams but those of his family and community as well. In his book of personal recollections *God Bless Our Home*, he reveals a deep respect for the traditions of the past and expresses hope that they will be preserved by succeeding generations of his family.

W.B. Greene was the cofounder of the Barber-Greene Company, a manufacturer of asphalt construction material. Located in Aurora, Illinois, the company that started in 1916 grew to international status and at one time had sales over $130 million and employed about 3,400 people. In 1966, its 50th anniversary year, Barber-Greene published the commemorative book *Our First Five Decades* in which W.B. Greene affirmed the guiding principle behind the company: "Our role has been to ease the burdens of mankind. Our machines dig the ditches, shovel the coal, build the roads, and do those dirty, rough, heavy jobs at one time assigned to our newest immigrants—the men with the shovels and the wheelbarrows."

W.B. Greene was photographed as a young child, probably around 1889, in clothes worn by baby boys and girls that at the time were mostly gender neutral (with the exception that girls' clothing had a little more eyelet or lace). Boys made the change to pants once they could easily undo the rather complicated fastenings of breeches and trousers. On seeing this photograph, W.B. Greene was known to remark that at least he did not have curls as a baby! In his own words from his book *Dear Progeny*: "I was born of poor but honest parents on September 4, 1886—'land poor,' at least—the third child of seven; the one following me died at birth. 'We Six' became a close-knit group, had loving parents and happy childhoods, with work enough to achieve a sense of purpose topped off with college educations paid for by the farm."

Above are W.B. Greene's paternal roots. From left to right are his uncle William D. Goodrich; William's wife, aunt Gertrude Hattie Greene (sister of William Spencer Greene); cousin Lue Morgan (daughter of his aunt Laura Eliza Greene and sister of William Spencer Greene); and his parents, Jessie Hibbard Greene and William Spencer Greene, all enjoying a warm sunny day alongside the farm. On the maternal side, his grandparents were Thomas Marsh Hibbard and Cleantha B. Storm. He called them Grandpapa and Grandmama to distinguish them from his paternal grandparents, Grandpa William Briggs Greene and Grandma Harriet Meeker Greene. William Spencer and Jessie Hibbard had a wonderful zest for life, a great capacity for work, and unparalleled energy and enthusiasm. It is never simple for two or three generations to live as one family, and life at Oak Cottage was one of harmony in the midst of surely everyday tensions.

This is a traditional photograph of W.B. Greene as a student at the University of Illinois in 1907. As the descendant of early settlers and a farmer who owned land, he recognized some of the advantages of prestige that he had in society. However, under the shadow of his exemplary older brother, he learned early on to fight for his rights. His first job as a janitor at Goodrich School may have laid the foundation for his industrious and meticulous approach to the world of business. After four years at Northwestern (now known as North Central College), he studied mechanical engineering at the University of Illinois. As an active member of the Phi Gamma Delta fraternity, he fine-tuned his leadership skills. When he realized that engineering education was too specialized and narrow for him, he delved into economics and the liberal arts. He graduated in 1910, in the wake of the 1907 depression.

Jane Smith became his bride in 1910 after a courtship that lasted over two years. W.B. Greene had met her earlier at a friend's house, was smitten by her captivating smile, and discovered that they had many things in common. However, Jane had to return to her home in Auburn, New York. In his senior year of college, he realized that he was in love and proposed to her by mail. She did not respond immediately, but he was persistent in his correspondence, and it paid off. He wanted to see her, but he first had to earn enough to pay for his fare to New York. He worked on the farm and finally saw her in 1908 on his 22nd birthday. Two years later, they were married. Jane's full name was Eva Jane Smith, named for her mother, who was presumed to have been named after Little Eva of *Uncle Tom's Cabin*.

W.B. Greene and Jane Greene had their first child, Maxson Hibbard Greene, in 1915; however, he tragically succumbed to an illness thought to be meningitis or something similar and died in 1922. Maxson was only seven at the time, and the pain of his loss was unbearable for the Greenes. Mortality rates were high for babies in the early 1900s, where about 30 percent did not survive past their fifth birthday. Together, W.B. Greene and Jane surmounted their grief over the loss of their promising first-born son, knowing that they had each other and their second child, Sally Jane, who was four at the time, to sustain them. They decided it would be best for all to have more children. Alex was born the following year, and Tony was born 18 months after that.

Sally Greene Mathews is shown here with two of her older sons, Stephen Maxson Mathews (right) and Peter Greene Mathews (left). She enjoyed 37 years of a wonderful marriage with Dr. Benton Mathews in California and became the mother of four boys. William Benton Mathews came nine years after Peter, and Joseph Dunnegan Mathews followed two years later. Sally's father, W.B. Greene, felt that she was life's gift to him and often fondly referred to her as "Skipper." Father and daughter had a lot in common; their values, philosophy, and goals in life were shared almost to perfection. Her giving attitude and the way she raised her boys earned his respect and brought much joy and pride to Greene. He penned a letter to his first unborn grandchild that read, "My dear Otto, I understand you have finally made a decision, selected your parents and the approximate date of arrival . . . And if you have been watching these past twenty-two years, the black-haired, blue-eyed beauty that became the rough tough tomboy, and then the whole combination together, you can believe that you have chosen well. So all welcome to you, Otto boy or girl—thrice welcome."

Pictured here are two sons of W.B. Greene and Jane Greene, William Alexander "Alex" Greene (right) and Anthony Storm "Tony" Greene (left). They were two years apart in age; Alex was born in 1923, followed by Tony in 1925. Both boys were in college at the University of Illinois when war broke out. They were young at the time and felt the urge to help their countrymen. Alex joined the Combat Engineers, one of the most hazardous of the services, and Tony served as second lieutenant in the Marines. But fate smiled on them, and peace was declared before they were called to engage in warfare. Tony was on board a ship in Boston Harbor and Alex was on his way to the front in Germany when the Germans had surrendered.

Here, W.B. Greene is sharing farm experiences with his teenage boys, Tony (left) and Alex. The boys had heard how their father as a lad had helped with haying, milking the cows, plowing the fields, harvesting and threshing the small grains, making ice cream in the icehouse, trimming the hedge fences, cultivating corn, and even laying shingles on the barn. W.B. Greene was delighted and comforted that his boys were growing up to be both considerate and concerned citizens. Alex became vice president and secretary of Barber-Greene. He, like his father, gave of his time and talents to the community, such as with the YMCA and Scouts, and served as chairman of the board of Aurora College. Tony worked at the Canadian plant of Barber-Greene for 10 years before he came back to Aurora and served as president and chairman of the board of the same, which had now grown to be one of the Fortune 500 companies.

This photograph is of a Christmas card sent to family and friends of the Greenes around 1936. Written by W.B. Greene, the poem "The Greene Humpty Dumpty" is artfully inscribed around the card and reads as follows:

Humpty Dumpty sat on a wall
With no one to hold him he had a great fall
If the whole Dumpty family
Had sat up together
King's horses and men
Would have been saved their bother

When Life's thorns and darts prick
Together we stick,
It's a hard combination to beat
So, we shoulder to shoulder
Grow older and bolder
And trouble turns down the side street.

Like ourselves? Bet we do!
But we like our friends too,
Or we wouldn't pose for such scenes—
So Happy New Year
And best Christmas Cheer
From every one of the Greenes.

Above, in 1935, the family of W.B. Greene is pictured in the backyard of their Frank Lloyd Wright–designed home. From left to right are Tony, William, Sally, Alex, and Jane Greene. Below is a street view of the home in Aurora after a winter snowstorm. The Greenes had been living in a second-floor apartment for two years when Jane suggested that they acquire their own house. Her thrifty household management skills enabled them to pull through hard times and live a happy and healthy life, enjoying one another, their family, the beauty of nature, and their many friends. They bought a lot on the far west of Aurora for a reasonable $750 and built their home on the property in 1912. Harry Robinson, an associate of Wright, made a series of sketches for their consideration. It was, according to them, "the house of our dreams." In 1915, they added a garage and acquired two lots adjacent to their home on 1300 Garfield Avenue in Aurora.

In 1959, when Jane Greene suffered a heart attack and wished for a smaller home, they prevailed upon their son Alex and his wife to occupy their home, and Jane and W.B. built and moved into a smaller dwelling in one of the adjacent lots at 111 South Gladstone Avenue in Aurora. The smaller house was built in the shadow of Aurora's only Frank Lloyd Wright home. The latter house was designed in a simple Usonian style, modern yet affordable with clean lines, skylights, hardwood floors, and built-in bookshelves. A solarium family room overlooks the backyard with winding flagstones surrounding gorgeous perennials.

W.B. Greene and his younger sister Grace are pictured in the Model T Ford that had been on the Greene farm since 1950 (it was stored in the barn). It is interesting to note that Grace is at the wheel, considering that she had not driven a Model T for about 50 years. Grace lived in Downers Grove for two years after her marriage to Everett Anson Brown but came back to the farm to care for her aging parents. She was like a little mother to all. Her loving exuberant spirit provided the security blanket that her parents and older siblings needed. Grace Greene Brown and Everett Anson Brown frequently hosted large family gatherings at Oak Cottage, keeping the family well connected and able to experience the wholesome living that life on a farm provides.

TO GRACE ON HER SIXTIETH

As I totter down life's road
Ahead of you, my little Sister,
Your feet still nimbly patter,
While mine blister...

Your cartwheels still astonish
Every grandchild,
While mine evoke
"There's Grandpa, piled!"

We bring you all our troubles
Which under you, become mere bubbles;
You keep the fire aglow on family hearth,
And ease our steps a-down Life's weary parth.

You're agile, while I'm fragile.
You're three-score, while I'm more.
You're good, while I'm better -
Or so you said in your nice letter.

You cheerily carry on your daily task
Your cheer, in fact, is all we ask.

While you should only sit and knit
You travel daily o'er the heaving floors.
You stop the breezes through the leaky doors.
You mop the drips -
You love us drips, in fact.

You're kind to all your elders
And your betters;
You raise our spirits - or at least
Send Everett for spirits.

Laura and I - we later wondered why -
Sat up all night and kept you from
A heavenly flight -
Now we know why.

Our dear little mother - little sister -
While you're flip, we slip
While you're gay, we bit the hay.

Oh youth, youth (with scarce a tooth)
We envy you and love you more -
At three score!

W.B.G. [illegible]/30/63

The Greene family is known to burst into poetry at any event for a variety of reasons, be it a birthday, coming of age, graduation, wedding anniversary, or even death. Here, W.B. Greene, then 77, eloquently shares his admiration for his sister Grace on her 60th birthday. Some excerpts from the poem, which is typed up on very fragile vintage paper, are as follows:

> As I tatter down life's road
> Ahead of you, my little Sister,
> Your feet still nimbly patter, While mine blister
>
> You're agile, while I'm fragile
> You're threescore, while I'm more
> You're good, while I'm better–
> Or so you said, in your letter.
>
> Our dear little mother–little sister–
> While you're flip, we slip
> While you're gay, we bit the hay
> Oh youth, youth (with scarce a tooth)
> We envy you and love you more–
> At three score!

Honoring W.B. Greene's wife, Jane Greene, at the dedication of the Girl Scout Building are, from left to right, William Alexander Greene with his wife, Marjory; W.B. Greene; Sally Greene Mathews; and Anthony Storm Greene with his wife, Barbara. W.B and Jane Greene had long sought a fitting way to share their family farm with others rather than selling to developers. They wished to maintain its beauty, keeping the open land free for the spirits of their ancestors to roam and to enjoy. After much care and consideration, in the 1960s, they gifted 136 acres of lovely dense rolling woodland, ravines, and pond just east of the Greene Valley Forest Preserve (east of Route 53 between Seventy-First and Seventy-Fifth) to the Girl Scouts. The area now known as Camp Greenwood, an open space of undisturbed natural beauty in the midst of a densely populated area, is maintained and cared for by the Girl Scouts of Greater Chicago and Northwest Indiana.

W.B. Greene and his daughter Sally Greene Mathews honor Jane Greene by recognizing her work and interest in the Girl Scouts organization with a plaque at the Girl Scout Building at Camp Greenwood. W.B. Greene and his wife, Jane, had recently returned from a pleasant trip to California when Jane suffered a stroke and a peaceful death on November 28, 1973. W.B. Greene and Jane had always felt that communion with nature, great symphonies, and great art was spiritually uplifting. W.B. Greene wrote in his book *Dear Progeny*: "When I meet St. Peter at the gate, I'll probably say, 'A little of each please.' Orthodox heaven with its streets of shining gold, sounds monotonous. We're still discovering those laws. I feel its presumptuous to pray for some personal advantage, except maybe a prayer for strength to carry out what we feel are His wishes."

Pictured from left to right are (first row) Ralph Batten, a good friend of the Greene family, and Arthur Greene; (second row) W.B. Greene and Hibbard Greene. Batten was a regular guest at Oak Cottage and was present at most special occasions such as Thanksgiving and Christmas. He was a little older than Hibbard, but his childish enthusiasm, akin to Barrie's Peter Pan, who never grew up, was contagious.

Pictured is Judith Greene Shepard flanked by her parents, William Alexander Greene (son of W.B. and Jane Greene) and Marjory Mather Greene. Judy married Dr. Chuck Shepard and had two sons, Peter and Chris.

Taken in Belvedere, California, in 1983, the above image shows, from left to right, William Benton Mathews (son of Sally Greene Mathews and Benton Mathews), his daughter Lindsey, and Sally, his mother. The photograph below shows Dr. Christopher Greene, a grandson of W.B. Greene, with his wife, Sarah, and daughter Jennifer. When W.B. Greene was asked for advice from one of his grandchildren in 1933, his response was, "Well, of course, the old platitudes still hold. They're as good as when I got them from my father, and he from his father. There is no substitute for hard work, character—honor or integrity—or deep thinking. . . . I only ask that you keep your perspective—your sense of humor—that your influence be always for the social good—that you judge not by financial achievement but by character—that you be not stampeded by old sentiments or new theories—that the zest of life be gathered day by day and not postponed for the future—and thus you will achieve a satisfaction that too few of my generation can attain."

Pictured at a Barber-Greene dinner in 1953 are Jane and W.B. Greene. The company was started in 1916 by Harry Barber and W.B. Greene, both of whom were employed at Stephens-Adamson at the time, an important local manufacturer of bulk moving machinery. Both had degrees in mechanical engineering, youthful passion, creativity and rigor, and wanted to make a difference in their world. They left Stephens-Adamson, started a partnership, and began Barber-Greene on October 21, 1916, with a $7,000 initial investment. Barber was the idea man, and Greene supervised sales and finances. The company closed three years after Greene passed away in 1982. His distinguished business career as founder and president of the Barber-Greene Company had all the ingredients of a hometown-boy-makes-good story.

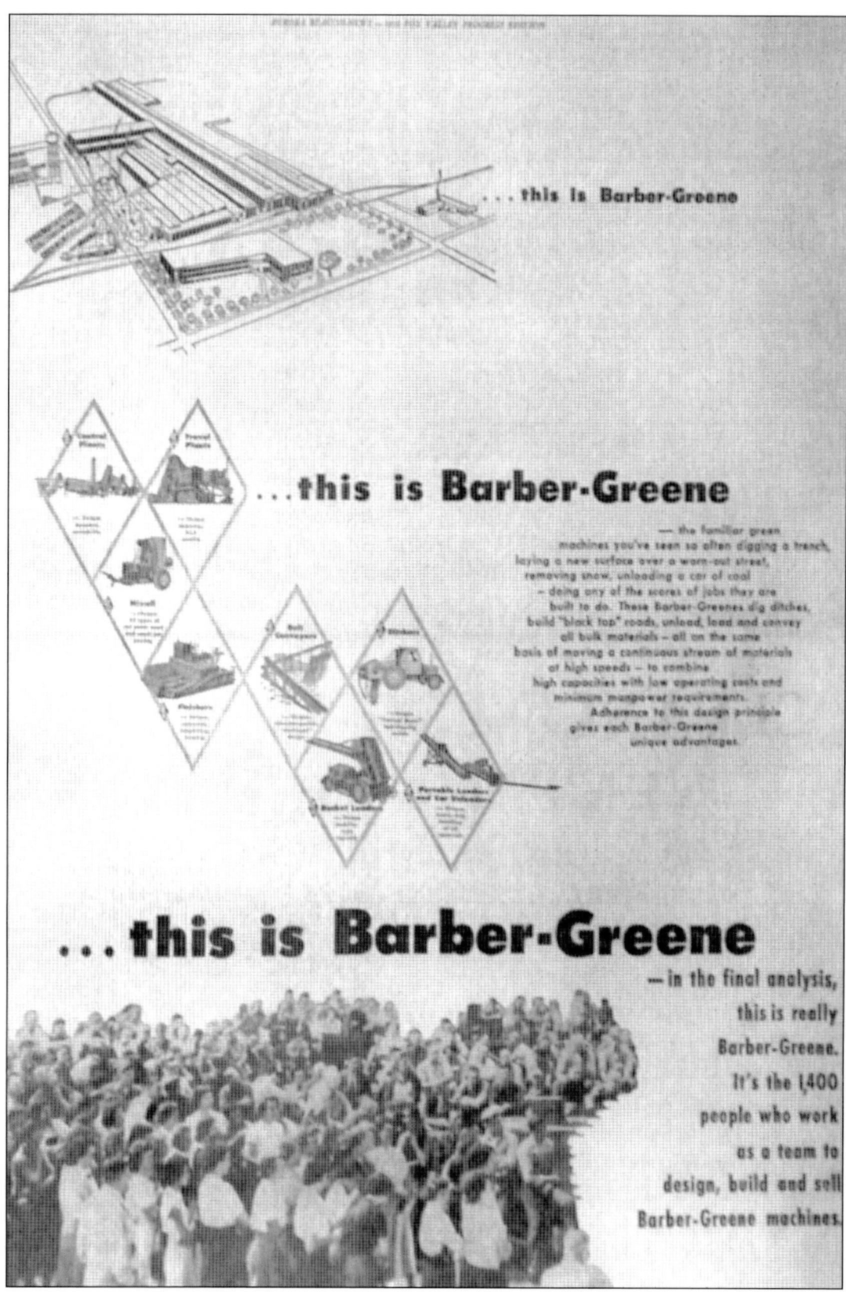

This advertisement featured the vast facility of the Barber-Greene Company, the various kinds of equipment that the company manufactured, and its most precious capital—the employees. As the poster claims, "In the final analysis, this is really Barber-Greene. It's the 1,400 people who work as a team to design, build and sell Barber-Greene machines." In 1976, company sales topped over $100 million. It had over 5,000 employees in its three US factories in Aurora, Elgin, and DeKalb and in its plants in Brazil, Canada, and England. W.B. Greene's primary objective was to ease the hard work that farmers faced in materials handling, such as digging, surfacing, and moving. Machines like the central pleats, travel pleats, Mixall, belt conveyors, basket loaders, ditchers, portable loaders, and car unloaders were invented to help ease those burdens.

This is an original solid metal belt buckle, a souvenir from the Barber-Greene Company. Featured in the buckle is an asphalt paver, a brainchild of Harry Barber. The machine was designed from a sketch drawn by Barber in 1930 in Aurora and patented in 1932. Defense contracts for highways and airports during World War II, along with increased demand for asphalt mixing and paving machines, catapulted the company into a multinational corporation employing thousands.

Here, W.B. Greene and his wife, Jane, ride in their favorite transport, a Ford Model T belonging to nephew Thomas Brown. This photograph was taken when W.B. Greene was ready to publish *Dear Progeny*. The backdrop for this famous photograph is the Greene barn, built by W.B. Greene's father, William Spencer Greene. The barn began to rise about the time that the first of the "We Six" was born, around 1882.

Here, W.B. Greene and his wife, Jane, are at an official opening of a new Barber-Greene factory in Bury, St. Edmunds, Suffolk, England. W.B. Greene is holding the ribbon-cutting scissors in his hand. At the time, Benford, a maker of construction equipment in England, was a client of Barber-Greene. As the Barber-Greene Company became a large and prosperous international complex, W.B. Greene's farsighted leadership as an organizer, administrator, financier, and inspiring leader of men was brought to light, which extended beyond his industry to civic and educational ventures and even to voluntary public service. Public schools, playgrounds, the Boy Scouts, Girl Scouts, Community Chest, Kiwanis, Aurora Foundation, Park District, YMCA, and YWCA all benefited from W.B. Greene's inspiring leadership and generosity. From 1949 to 1955, W.B. Greene was president of the construction industry's Manufacturer's Association and served as director of the American Road Builders' Association, International Road Federation, and Illinois State Chamber of Commerce.

The mutual love and respect between W.B. Greene and his wife, Jane Greene, endured for 63 years until Jane's death in 1973. They had stood together through happy and tragic times. They shared the risks of a new business and rode out the fury of the Great Depression. He had married an independent young woman with strong convictions. She had good intuition, and W.B. Greene was known to rely on her judgement of people. They read a great deal together, enjoying the same books, movies, and plays. However, the greatest bond they cherished was their home life and their children. W.B. Greene often said that the years with his growing family were their golden years. They both enjoyed travel and were curious and eager to learn from the different value systems around the world. They visited Europe via the *Queen Mary* in 1949, South America in 1954, the Near East in 1955, and the Orient in 1960.

A birthday cake with one lit candle waits for W.B. Greene. His business venture, the Barber-Greene Company, entered a golden phase of rapid and profitable growth for about 20 years, from 1946 to 1966. These years coincided with the end of World War II and the postwar boom in highway construction in the United States. Much of the growth was also due to his organized sales efforts, creation of international partnerships, and the new machines created by Harry Barber. Jack Turner, a longtime associate, wrote, "There is absolutely no way that I could write anything that would truly convey to someone else the wit, wisdom, principles, humor, compassion, empathy, insight, broad viewpoint, etc., etc. of W.B. Greene. I had the privilege of working closely, intimately with him for many years. It was a gratifying, often inspiring experience."

In this photograph, W.B. Greene displays on his lap one of three books that he wrote, *God Bless Our Home*. His success as an industrialist never diminished his family ties or his fondness for Oak Cottage and its surrounding acres. Even while he was president and chairman of the board of Barber-Greene, he found time to publish three books in his own words for his "Dear Grandchildren and Unknown Great-grandchildren." *The Greenes on the East Branch of the DuPage* (1966) traced the lines of his ancestry and included letters from his grandmother written in 1845. Recollections of his boyhood at Oak Cottage were captured in *God Bless Our Home* (1977), the title taken from the blessing fashioned from leaves and grains by his grandmother more than a century earlier. *Dear Progeny* (1979) supplemented his biographical record with details on his education, business endeavors, civic contributions, and much more.

W.B. Greene celebrates his 90th birthday at Oak Cottage in 1976 with family and friends. For this occasion, his sister Laura's daughter Gingy Wheeler wrote this citation titled "Vintage":

To Achieve This—
A wine should be laid on its side, in the dark, But not for you,
A car should be polished, tinkered, pampered, tuned, But not for you.
A man of vintage status
Who's done his jogging, physical and mental
Who's built his castles, not just dreamed them
Who's bonded his family, not just charted them
There's a man who's won his Blue Ribbon
Truly the Best of Vintage.

Even in his post-retirement days, he continued to devote himself to civic causes, the environment, and increased dependence on technology. His private secretary, Alberta Schiltz, was able to complement his failing short-term memory and preference for generalities versus details, while helping him with charitable activities that he conducted from his office.

For most of his 95 years, W.B. Greene's recitation of Eugene Field's famous poem "Jest 'fore Christmas" has entertained the Oak Cottage crowd at Christmastime. The tradition continues; it is perhaps the family's oldest uninterrupted custom. It reads as follows:

Father calls me William, sister calls me Will,
Mother calls me Willie, but the fellers call me Bill!
Mighty glad I ain't a girl—ruther be a boy,
Without them sashes, curls, an' things that's worn by Fauntleroy!
Love to chawnk green apples an' go swimmin' in the lake—
Hate to take the castor-ile they give for bellyache!
Most all the time, the whole year round, there ain't no flies on me,
But jest 'fore Christmas I'm as good as I kin be!

For Christmas, with its lots an' lots of candies, cakes, an' toys,
Was made, they say, for proper kids an' not for naughty boys;
So wash yer face an' bresh yer hair, an' mind yer p's and q's,
An' don't bust out yer pantaloons, and don't wear out yer shoes;
Say "Yessum" to the ladies, and "Yessur" to the men,
An' when they's company, don't pass yer plate for pie again;
But, thinkin' of the things yer'd like to see upon that tree,
Jest 'fore Christmas be as good as yer kin be!

W.B. Greene died peacefully on February 6, 1982. The Barber-Greene Company created this poster at his passing and issued a very fitting announcement: "It is with deep sorrow that we announce the passing of our co-founder, former Chairman and President William B. Greene on February 6, 1982. His inspiring leadership and wisdom advanced his company, his community, and his industry. Born near Lisle, Illinois, September 4, 1886, he graduated from the University of Illinois with Bachelor of Science degree in Mechanical Engineering in 1908. He maintained an interest and involvement in the university throughout the years. Greene continued in active management of the company until 1966 when he retired as Chairman of the Board. He continued to be active until recently." Just five months earlier, he had celebrated his 95th birthday with his children, nine grandchildren, great-grandchildren, his sister Grace, and various nieces, nephews, cousins, in-laws, and extended family—about 40 all told. The party was held in the big yard between his house and his son Alex's home in Aurora. He sat in his big chair on the terrace and was surrounded by admirers and two huge bulletin boards with letters, poems, and cards from all over the country.

This is one of the last photos of W.B. Greene and his younger sister Grace Greene Brown on the front steps of Oak Cottage. After his wife Jane's passing in 1973, W.B. was finding it increasingly difficult to adjust to life without her at his home in Aurora. His office continued to be his sanctuary and a welcome distraction. Grace had previously lost her husband, Everett, in October 1968 and was living alone while managing Oak Cottage. On Grace's request, he moved back to Oak Cottage and found that they were better off together than separate and alone. He would drive the 17-mile commute from Oak Cottage to his office every day until his own ill health very close to his end would not permit him to operate a car. W.B. Greene's home in Aurora continued to be his official address, and he would stay overnight there to attend any evening meetings. Nancy Hibbard Brown (daughter of Grace Greene Brown) and several caregivers took care of Grace while she was recovering from a pacemaker implant. W.B. Greene stayed by his sister until her passing on Christmas Day in 1981, and he himself succumbed to cancer six weeks later. *An extraordinary era had come to an end.*

Five

The Barn Renaissance

Speaking of old buildings, they are not just ours.
They partly belong to those who built them
and partly to all generations of mankind
who are to follow us.

—John Ruskin

There is something magical about old timber frame barns. They represent more than simply wood and stone, portraying a critical part of America's heritage and cultural values. It is about the history behind the construction, the experiences of the family who owned them, a bridge to the past. Barns tell stories of hard work, dedication, tradition, aspiration, innovation, and community. They remind us of a simpler time, of warmth and life, and of a place to shelter from the harsh elements of the Midwest prairie. To preserve a barn is to keep this one-of-a-kind story alive for all to see, touch, and experience.

The word *barn* comes from the Old English *bere*, for barley or grain, and *aern*, a storage place, translating to a "storehouse for grain." The prairie barn was built to store a large amount of hay and grain and to keep farm animals snug and safe during cold hard winters. The first immigrants, mostly from England and continental Europe, built their barns using the English barn as the prototype, with stucco-like walls. As settlers acquired land, they harvested timber to use as a building material or fuel, or simply cleared the land for crops and pasture. Farmers quickly adapted, covering roofs and sidewalls with horizontal or vertical wooden planks. With the heightened interest in dairy farming and greater livestock production, animal stables were built along either side of the barn.

The Greene family barn was constructed in three sections around 1880 and is now owned and maintained by the Forest Preserve District of DuPage County. Naperville citizens recognized the cultural treasure they had in their midst and took measures to secure the barn's stabilization in 2011–2012. Support for the full restoration of the barn and Oak Cottage has been growing ever since. The hope is that this venerable homestead will be enjoyed by the public not only as a welcoming, magnificent gathering space but also as an informative window into DuPage County's agricultural past.

This is the beloved stately Greene family barn prior to stabilization. It stands proudly at the corner of Hobson and Greene Roads along the East Branch of the DuPage River and is a landmark of the farm heritage of Naperville in DuPage County, Illinois. This nearly 14,000-square-foot barn, constructed as a great storehouse for the bounty of the land, is the largest in the county and still has its first silo inside. The barn began to rise around 1880, a timber frame structure with

quarry stone for its foundation. It is a simple yet practical expression of a people, a pioneer way of life, and the prairie assets from which it was built. This venerable structure evokes a sense of the energy, the beauty, and the traditions embedded in its magnificent space. (Courtesy of Forest Preserve District of DuPage County.)

If only this barn could talk! These pictures show what the ravages of time and neglect can do to these extraordinary structures. In the late 20th century, after more than a century since its construction, the barn gradually sank into decay, the silos were worn down by the weather, and the wood cracked as rain seeped into the barn along with mold and small animals. In addition, water, dust, and organic matter that collected at the rafter feet began to rot the timbers. Vines took a firm hold and crawled up the sides of the barn and the silo. Moisture leaking into the wood started breaking the bonds between the red paint and the wood fiber and accelerated the peeling of paint. Preventing the rapid decay of this historical treasure is entrusted to current and upcoming generations. (Both, courtesy of Forest Preserve District of DuPage County.)

In the spring of 2011, much to the delight of the community, a sign announcing the planned stabilization of the barn was placed at the corner of Hobson and Greene Roads in Naperville, Illinois. The hard hat on the fence was confirmation that efforts were indeed underway to save the barn from ultimate ruin. In 2010, an engineering and design services firm was brought in to provide input as to remedial actions that could be taken to save the barn. The barn preservation list was long, including the installation of steel beams, rebuilding the leaky roof, and creating spaces designed to be user friendly for everyone. Stabilization funds of approximately $1.2 million were designated from the Greene Family Forest Preserve Endowment Fund and a general Greene Valley improvement fund. Led by Rick Collins of Trillium Dell, a timber frame and restoration company, the improvements began. (Both photographs by the author.)

Here, the rafters on the oldest part of the barn have been exposed. W.B. Greene wrote, "Cordwood from land clearing was hauled to Naperville as a cash crop, and the return haul carried heavy stone from the Naperville quarries." Pine and oak trees were cut and milled locally. Most of the roof decking planks and rafters were replaced, and some were salvaged. The timber frame was assembled in one of the many grand barn raisings by members of the community, neighbors, and friends, who all helped one another. (Courtesy of Forest Preserve District of DuPage County.)

Gazing at the clouds on a cool spring day through the rafters, which run from the ridge of the roof to the rafter plate, is a unique experience. One is surprised by the massive open space, which is not very evident with a covered roof. (Photograph by the author.)

In the above photograph, the rafter plates have extensive damage. Where possible, time-honored techniques that are hundreds of years old such as mortise tenon joinery and wooden pegs were used by the team during the restoration. Internal splines as well as epoxy were used to repair the rafter plates and posts. Because of the extensive decay, several original rafters were replaced with newly stained white oak rafters that matched the original color. (Photograph by the author.)

This photograph shows work being done to restore the roof of the milk house, an addition which originally used white pine sourced from Michigan. The milk house processed 27 eight-gallon cans of milk per day, which was an astonishing feat for a farm at the time, and employed many hands. In W.B Greene's book *God Bless Our Home*, he estimates that they had shipped close to 12 billion quarts of milk to the Chicago market during a period of 100 years. (Photograph by the author.)

Pictured here is the removal of the two four-sided original cupolas from their base, gently lowered onto the ground using a crane, and finally loaded onto a truck for transport to the Trillium Dell timber frame workshop, where they were to be replicated. The louvers of the cupolas were covered by plywood boards and strapped to protect them from damage during the removal process. Cupolas allow for ventilation of the haymow, with a continuous flow of air helping to dry the hay and keep it from rot and decay. Incidentally, the word cupola is derived from the Latin *cupa* or "small cup," indicating a vault or an upside-down cup. (Both photographs by the author.)

The above photograph shows the newly fabricated cupolas, which have arrived at the barn site. A 30-ton crane transported the cupolas to the roof of the barn, where two men guided and fastened them to the structure. Shown at right is the view of the same cupola installation from Greene Road, on the west side of the barn. W.B. Greene felt that the barn became, in his words, "a harmonious whole, balanced beautifully with the large cupolas, topped with lightning rods and wind vanes, one a horse, one a cow." The holes in the cupolas and barn walls allowed birds such as pigeons to enter the barn. The birds helped curb the population of flying insects inside the barn while contributing to the farmers food supply as needed. It was much easier to catch a pigeon when it was inside the barn than one flying in the sky. (Both photographs by the author.)

This view from the west of the barn shows the crane transporting the cupola to the main roof ridge; the two cupolas are approximately 56 feet apart. The original timber framed structure, an *L*-shaped building with each leg measuring 100 feet long, was built as a threshing barn with the haymow and grain bin on the top floor. The ramp from the top floor slopes down to the exterior grade level facing Hobson Road. As the farm continued to prosper, the structure was expanded with four sheds. (Photograph by the author.)

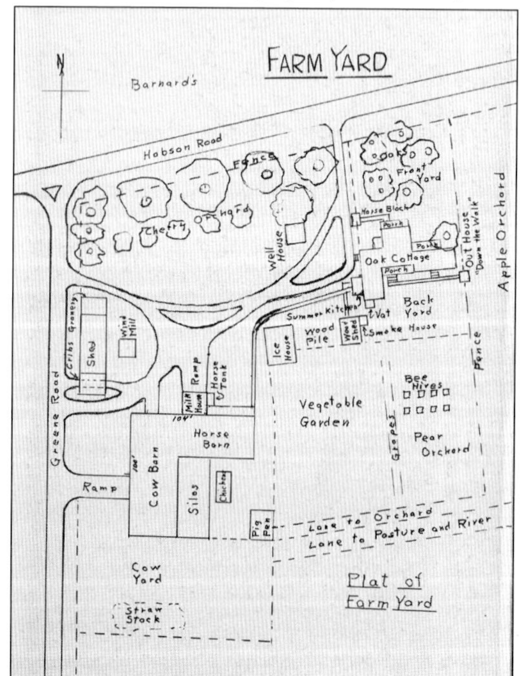

At left, the farm yard drawing by Thomas Everett Brown on the inside cover of *The Greenes on the East Branch of the DuPage* depicts the additions made over time. A corn crib, a wagon shed, a granary, a pigpen, and a chicken house along with a square wooden silo joined the wood shed, icehouse, well house, windmill, and smokehouse on the property.

These photographs display the supplies that were accumulated on the grounds of the barn as the stabilization continued. The planks in the foreground are roof decking and siding that were removed. Efforts were made to maintain the integrity of the century-old construction as much as possible within current material and funding constraints. Unfortunately, many of the original rafters could not be salvaged and had to be replaced with new white oak pieces, which were stained to match the original color. The siding planks that were stripped are from the lower areas close to the floor decking, where accumulated moisture and organic materials caused rot and decay. Planks used for scaffolding are stacked up in the picture below. (Both photographs by the author.)

The photograph at left shows a worker atop a manlift patching cracks in one of the concrete silos with epoxy. The Greene barn was the first in DuPage County to have a silo *inside* the barn. The first exterior concrete silo was built in 1915. American farm silos of the late 1800s and early 1900s were made of wood or stone. Interestingly, the word *silo* has origins in Spanish, derived from Geek *siros* or "a pit to keep corn in." Today, three concrete silos stand by the barn. One is a concrete stave silo constructed with interlocking masonry units reinforced with exterior, galvanized steel hoops, which provide the necessary tension for structural integrity. The other two are seamless concrete silos and have the reinforcement within the concrete itself. The photograph below reveals the dark gash on one of the silos, from where the compromised enclosure for the ladder was removed and subsequently replaced. (Both photographs by the author.)

The decayed silo tops were replaced with new aluminum dome roofs, as shown above. The old wooden silos with square corners that promoted rot were quickly displaced by round silos. These round silos enclosed more space using less material and were structurally suited to withstand the high pressures exerted by tons of stacked silage. The very first silo on the farm and in the county was a brainchild of William Spencer Greene and paid for itself in the first year. A rectangular structure about 30 by 70 feet with five separate rooms was built into the *L* of the barn. Each room had a doorway to the barn. Filling was done with a silage cutter, which fed silage into an inclined conveyor above the silo rooms. Horsepower was used to keep the conveyor moving. A worker inside distributed the silage and tamped it down to make it as airtight as possible. Hired hands would carry heavy baskets filled with silage to the mangers. The photograph below shows the view from the floor of the silo looking upward. (Above, photograph by the author; below, courtesy of Mary Lou Wehrli.)

Above is a view of the second-floor interior, a majestic sight with its hand-hewn timbers, both horizontal beams and vertical posts. The eye is drawn from the floor to the spectacular height of the central space. A sense of awe sets in as one takes in the colors of the well-worn boards, the miracle of the barn framing held together by mortice and tenon joints, and all this amidst the lingering smell of hay and grain. The rafters appear to have been salvaged, as they look darker than the timber frame and the roof decking boards installed over these rafters. Visible in the photograph below is the gable on the east side below the roof system of the main barn. (Both photographs by the author.)

These two images show the different stages of progress on the siding on the south side of the barn. In the above photograph, the gable end and the associated rafters have been removed and vertical boards have been installed with two-inch- to three-inch-wide battens added. The added battens cover the seams and seal the gaps between the boards, providing much-needed protection from the elements. About two-thirds of the way up in the photograph below, one can see that the upper vertical boards overlap the lower boards, again for extra weather protection. The cows were housed in the south wing of the barn, which had three rows of wooden stanchions with a capacity to house 90 Holsteins. The northeast wing of the barn with 16 stalls housed the horses, calves, and the bull. (Both photographs by the author.)

The above photograph shows a door opening that has been temporarily shored up while the limestone walls are being repaired. The photograph below shows a mason mixing up a traditional lime putty mortar, a mix of three ingredients—lime, sand, and water—to repoint a hand-quarried original limestone block. The repaired blocks will be used to reinforce weak spots in the foundation. Much of the quarried limestone may have come from what is known today as Centennial Beach in Naperville. (Both photographs by the author.)

The above photograph shows the west side of the ramp that is being reinforced, with Oak Cottage visible in the background. The ramp was used as an approach to the second floor, where the hay was brought and packed into the haymow area. Extensive stonework was required to repair the ramp and some sections of the walls. The stonework was repointed using lime putty mortar similar in composition to what was predominantly in use in the late 1800s, which also minimized damage to the century-old stones. In the photograph below, a truck-mounted crane stands ready to do some heavy lifting. (Both photographs by the author.)

Shown here is the lower level of the barn, which was reinforced with steel beams to hold up the upper floor decking and the roof systems. This area was originally partitioned to hold the farm animals, with trenches engineered to separate the hay and grain from the manure and the water bin. The smell inside could be overwhelming at times, with a mixture of hay, dust, manure, animals, feed silage, sweat, and wood all mixed together. (Courtesy of Mary Lou Wehrli.)

The Forest Preserve District of DuPage County approved the stabilization work in an effort to preserve as much of the original barn as possible. The handprints on the concrete, which belonged to Tom Everett Brown (son of Grace Greene Brown and Everett Anson Brown) when he was a young boy, were left untouched during the restoration. The imprint of his young hands, an important nostalgic relic from the past, is cherished by the entire Greene family and the community. (Courtesy of Mary Lou Wehrli.)

These photographs show the restored barn, resplendent in fresh red paint, standing strong and proud after more than a century and a half. The above photograph shows the north entrance to the barn via a ramp, while the view of the *L*-shaped barn from the east is pictured below. The future of the structure is not known at this juncture, but the vast interior space is a clarion call for usage as a public indoor space. (Both photographs by the author.)

This two-animal yoke or a team yoke is positioned upside down on a step. It is a long beam of wood with a curved notch at either end, one for each animal. In the early 1800s, a farmer would use a single walking plow pulled by a team of horses to prepare the ground for planting. Animals such as oxen, donkeys, or mules were also used to offset the manual labor. This changed dramatically in the 1940s during World War II as food production became a priority and gasoline-powered tractors were used to plow the fields. This yoke, a longtime relic, hung on the porch of Oak Cottage for many years. The ring shown below was a very important barn detail back in the day when horses were used for transportation, pulling sleighs and carriages, and for working the fields. Multiple rings embedded in thick limestone foundations were commonly found to tie animals to while harnessing or to prevent them from straying. (Both photographs by the author.)

Six

The Greene Family Legacy

The purpose of life is not to be happy. It is to be useful, to be honorable, to be compassionate, to have it make some difference that you have lived and lived well.

—Ralph Waldo Emerson

Leaving a legacy takes faith, drive, and consistency. William Bertram Greene did just that. He left an enduring legacy for his family and for the whole of humanity. W.B. Greene had an abiding sense of goodness and the creative passion to seek ways to enable a better and more peaceable world and community for everyone, and he took actions in his life towards these ends.

He published three books during his life, *The Greenes on the East Branch of the DuPage*, *God Bless Our Home*, and *Dear Progeny*, that were principally for the benefit of the Greene clan but have a much wider appeal. The books are full of warmth and wisdom and provide a window into his ancestry, his life experiences, and perspectives in the changing world around him as he progressed from childhood to old age. He writes, "It is my feeling that all humankind are entitled to the story of their ancestors—that human bloodlines are as deserving of record as those of our domestic animals." Copies of his books, including electronic versions, are available at Naperville Public Libraries and the Naperville Heritage Society.

In 1965, operations on the Greene farm ceased after 115 years with the auction of the dairy herd and renting of the fields for sod farming. In 1970, W.B. Greene generously gifted the Greene family's 10-acre homestead, including Oak Cottage and the 14,000-square-foot barn, to the Aurora Foundation (now known as the Community Foundation of the Fox River Valley), who, by prearrangement, sold it to the Forest Preserve District of DuPage County. The sale was completed in 1971 with the proceeds of $70,000 (establishing the Greene Family Forest Preserve Endowment Fund) to be used for the maintenance of the buildings. Additionally, he ensured that his younger sister Grace Greene Brown would have life tenancy at Oak Cottage. Not only did he leave a magnificent legacy for his family, but he also left a record of what it means to be decent and honorable, a person of high integrity who has genuine caring for his fellow man.

A Christmas wreath and festive lights on the Greene barn beckon memories of generations of the Greene family who worked, played, danced, laughed, cried, wed, worshipped, and celebrated life. For more than a century, the barn was witness to a pioneer family who built a home and a dairy farm that was the best in all of DuPage County. W.B. Greene had a wish: He wanted the homestead to be an example of early American life, a memory that the younger Greene generations could cherish and honor and one of which the public could have knowledge. In his own words, "Christmas is a reminder of Christ's spirit and teaching of goodwill to all mankind—to the poor of the Third World, and to those in your own backyard; not so much by material gifts as by your help in reorganizing the world for a better sharing of its goods and opportunities—for your unselfish wisdom in knowing who and what to support toward such end. If such is 'merry,' then Merry Christmas!" (Courtesy of Mary Lou Wehrli.)

The first annual meeting of the Aurora Foundation was held on November 23, 1948, at the office of the Aurora Chamber of Commerce. W.B. Greene, seated fifth from the left, was senior director from 1948 to 1982. He was the first president and director of the charitable organization that was formed by a group of volunteers. Since 1948, the foundation has awarded more than $20 million in scholarships. Aurora, a city just west of Naperville, was indeed fortunate in having civic-minded corporations such as the Aurora Foundation involved in activities that benefited the community. Donors from Barber-Greene and other civic-minded businesses and organizations found it beneficial to channel their contributions through the foundation. (Courtesy of Greg Probst, Community Foundation of the Fox River Valley.)

Oak Cottage
Family Picnic
On the 4th of July 1982

Find out who will win the Grace Brown Horse Shoe Championship!

Fun!

Wade in the mighty Dupage!

Have your picture taken by Tom's Model-T

Drink Eat Be Merry!

Games!

From the East coast

RAIN OR SHINE

To the West Coast

Everybody's Welcome!

For so many years, Oak Cottage has been the grand and gracious hostess of our family's gatherings. She has played an important role in the story of our family; a home which has inspired an interest in our heritage. We are happy for the opportunity of spending another holiday there in each other's company. In order to plan the picnic, we'd like to know how many people plan to attend. We need this information As soon as possible! (by May 15 latest.) Please fill this out, fold along the dotted line with the return address facing out, and mail.

☐ Yes, we are planning to attend – How many ________

Signed ________________

Thanks

A grand event, a family reunion of multiple generations, needs a grand invite, and that is what is portrayed here. An era had sadly ended at Oak Cottage with the passing of Grace Greene Brown at the age of 78 on Christmas Day in 1981. W.B. Greene also passed barely six weeks later. The Greene clan was shaken and needed to grieve, get together, reminisce, and display family solidarity to honor their ancestors. The family gathering would be a last hurrah of sorts, a pause to let each member pay homage to the values that were instilled in them by the "We Six" generation. A family reunion was planned by Betsy Greene and Nancy Stoneberg for the Fourth of July 1982 at Oak Cottage, and every member of the Greene family was invited. Tom and Nancy, the children of Grace, took over the immense job of getting the old homestead to look its best for the huge gathering. The Model T belonging to Tom Brown would be a major attraction, taking family members around the barn and into the woods where past generations had picnicked and played. The genealogical charts were tacked onto the Oak Cottage entrance, carrying back both the Greene and Hibbard lines to the 7th century AD.

A grand family reunion, with 73 members in attendance, was held at Oak Cottage on July 4, 1982. Members of all branches of the Greene family, the progeny of William Briggs Greene and Harriet Meeker Greene (descendants of Laura Greene Morgan, Gertrude Greene Goodrich, and William Spencer Greene), came from all corners of the country. Life at Oak Cottage always carried a nostalgic sense of security and shelter. Family members, however far away they lived from the homestead, "came back to the farm" and expressed their solidarity. Pictured are, from left to right, (children in the first row) Dan Ross, Tom Ross, Chip Ross, Ginny Ross, Liberty Greene, and Melissa Greene; (second row, kneeling or sitting) Bill Wilson, Marcia Wilson, Susan

Douthit, Evan Douthit (lying), Lue Douthit, John Ross, Judy Ross, Richard Greene, Mason Ross, Julie Ross, Tad Greene, Debbie Greene, Darrell Issa, Gordon Greene, Bill Stoneberg III, Sandy Stoneberg, and Everett Trygve Brown; (third row) Jim Wilson, Carol Jordan, Mary Ann Wilson, Bob Jordan, Mary Douthit, Hal Douthit, Bob Greene, Helen Ross, Betsy Greene, Gary Bauman, Cindy Greene, Betty Monning, Barbara Monning, Kathy Issa (holding Will Issa), Gingy Williams, Alex Greene, Marjorie Etnyre, Tony Greene, Barb Greene, Bill Stoneberg, Nancy Stoneberg, Chris Stoneberg (holding Dan Stoneberg), Dave Stoneberg, Pete Stoneberg, Tom Brown, Peggy Brown, Bill Thompson, and Vera Dell Thompson.

The Greene family took the initiative to create a newsletter so that expanding family members, scattered across all continents, could keep in touch and communicate. W.B. Greene's older sister Laura Belvedera Greene had been the family correspondent, the glue that held the extended family together, until her passing in 1977. She had been a witty, wise, and sensitive reporter of the doings of the Greene kinsfolk for 70–80 years, even keeping track of second and third cousins. Robert Spencer Greene, the nephew of W.B. Greene and son of Hibbard Spencer Greene, was the creator of the newsletter, which was named *Now and Then*. It was published from 1979 to 1985, then sporadically thereafter. Robert's daughter Elizabeth "Betsy" Hibbard Greene picked up the torch in 1994.

Off My Rocker

. . . . by EHG

In the last several years we have suffered the losses of our beloved Helen Greene Ross, Gingy Wheeler Williams, and creator and first editor of "Now and Then", Bob Greene. They will leave a huge hole in all of us never to be filled the same way again. Such is the case of all who go before us. As the 4th generation of the "Oak Cottagers" dwindles, the 5th and 6th generations are growing. We 5th's are now moving into the position that our parents and their parents before them, ad infinitum, held; that is: of being the "grownups". We have been very fortunate to have been left a rich and well recorded heritage. A saga of an American Family which was so very carefully and lovingly kept and added to and passed on. This is something most families don't have. This is a story we should hand to our children as it was handed to us. With the leaving of Oak Cottage as our central meeting place, we had to create a new Oak Cottage. One in our hearts and one on paper. "Now and Then" is our Oak Cottage on paper. So, what shall we do? Shall we let it slide? Or shall we keep it alive? It's up to US, my fellow cousins. What is needed here is participation. If you care, then show it. Send in your dues, respond to the issue, send in ideas, photos, or stories. Show it to your kids. Get them interested. We need a 6th generation reporter as well. This could be the glue that sticks a very large and diverse family together, if we want it. So let me know if I'm on the right track, or just off my rocker.

Betsy

Above is a plea from Betsy Hibbard Greene to the entire clan in the 1997 edition of *Now and Then* to continue to honor the tradition of family communications and closeness, in her words, "to create a new Oak Cottage, one in our hearts, and one on paper," as the keys of Oak Cottage had been turned over to the Forest Preserve District of DuPage County in July 1983. Earlier, in the 1994 edition, when Robert Spencer Greene was asked to state the purpose of the newsletter, he wrote, "I discovered a common strain of decency, honesty, integrity, and a willingness to work hard, both for the family and the community. Nothing that rates headlines, certainly, but qualities that contribute to the building of a better family, community, world. I find that admirable, and worth preserving. And I hope that *Now and Then* can play a part in keeping these qualities as part of our lives now, as they were in the lives of our forebears."

Pictured from left to right are Herb Nadelhoffer (a farm neighbor of the Greenes) and Thomas Everett Brown, who were good friends throughout the years and passionate about saving the Greene farmstead. Herb and Woodridge volunteer Joni Mimnaugh dedicated countless hours highlighting the many possible uses by the public for Oak Cottage and the barn. Tom Brown and his sister Nancy Hibbard Brown also helped in negotiations with the Forest Preserve District of DuPage County officials and the Naperville Heritage Society. (Courtesy of Mary Lou Wehrli.)

Mary Lou Wehrli (spouse of Herb Nadelhoffer) is pictured with architecture students from Naperville School District 203 high schools who toured the barn to learn construction complexities and draw attention to the adaptive reuse of the barn. As a commissioner in the Forest Preserve District of DuPage County, Mary Lou Wehrli led several initiatives to educate and involve the citizens of Naperville so that the barn would always be a part of the area's landscape. (Courtesy of Mary Lou Wehrli.)

The above photograph was taken in August 1985 at *Sunday in the Country*, a special event staged on the Greene property with Oak Cottage as the backdrop. A script was written and directed by Herb Nadelhoffer, starring, among others, Jane Sindt and Kay Stephens from the Naperville Heritage Society, Tad and Betsy Greene, Tom and Anne Brown, Herb Nadelhoffer, and Mary Lou Wehrli playing various illustrious Greene forebears. The afternoon was filled with historical facts amidst poetry and folk music. The audience was treated to skits wherein actors depicting various Greene family characters ascended the stage to tell their stories. The event was a great success and was followed by sequels in 1986 and 1987. Tours of Oak Cottage, food, games, period costumes, old cars, and horse carriages, as shown in the photograph below, were icing on the cake. *Sunday in the Country* was based on Chautauqua events that were popular in the late 19th and early 20th centuries, as they brought entertainment and culture to the whole community with showmen, musicians, speakers and specialists of the day. Former US president Theodore Roosevelt was quoted as saying that Chautauqua was "the most American thing in America." (Both, courtesy of Mary Lou Wehrli.)

These two photographs were taken at the Rooted Acoustic Barn Raising (RABR) events that were held every year starting in August 2019. The Forest Preserve District of DuPage County agreed to open the Greene barn to the public for one day to support ongoing efforts to raise funds and build awareness for this striking cultural treasure. A 5K and one-mile dash, along with face painting, food, music, plein air art, and gift certificates, provide fun for all ages. Activities related to health, education, art, music, and gifts of nature help to highlight the multifaceted potential usage of the barn as a public space and increase community support. The Greene Barn Ad-Hoc Committee, chaired by Rachel Jenness, was created by the Forest Preserve District board in January 2019. The committee made a phased set of recommendations that emphasized efficient and effective investment of district appropriations while allowing vigorous complementary revenue streams to facilitate public utilization of the barn. (Both, courtesy of Mary Lou Wehrli.)

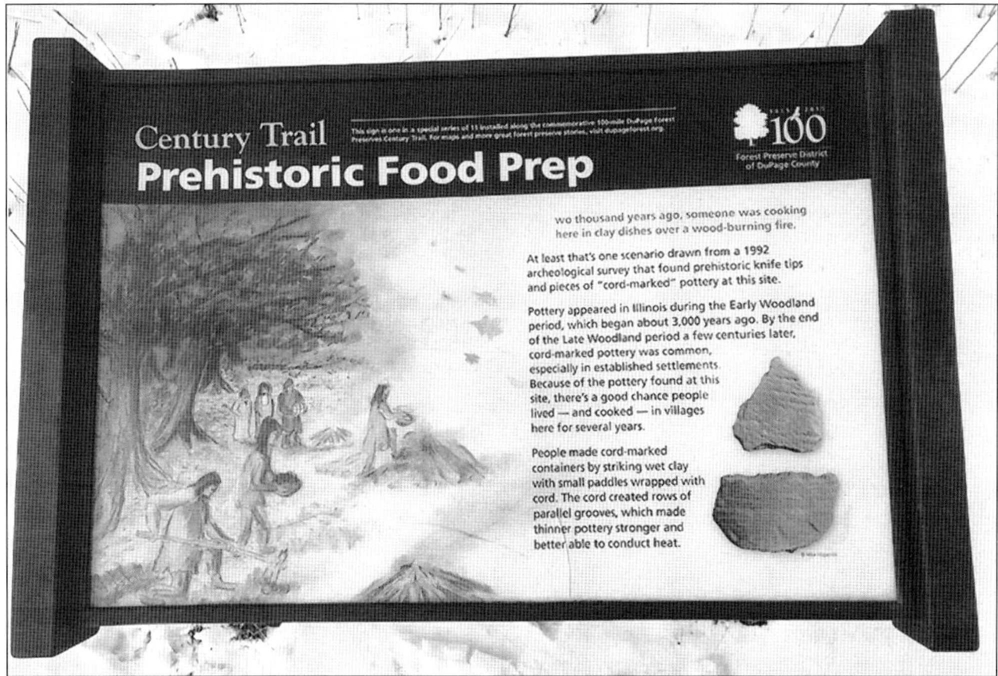

The historic marker shown above is installed in the Greene Valley Forest Preserve and is evidence of Native American tribes who used stone tools and cord-marked pottery for food preparation. The historic marker below is the Indian Boundary Line, part of a treaty in 1816 that established a safe corridor for European settlers and traders moving west. The treaty between the US government and the Native American tribes of the area—the Ojibwe, Ottawa, and Potawatomi, known as the Council of Three Fires—delineated a 20-by-70-mile strip of land that stretched from Lake Michigan southwest to the Illinois River near present-day Ottawa. The northern border of the Indian Boundary Line goes right through the Greene Valley Forest Preserve. (Both, courtesy of Mary Lou Wehrli.)

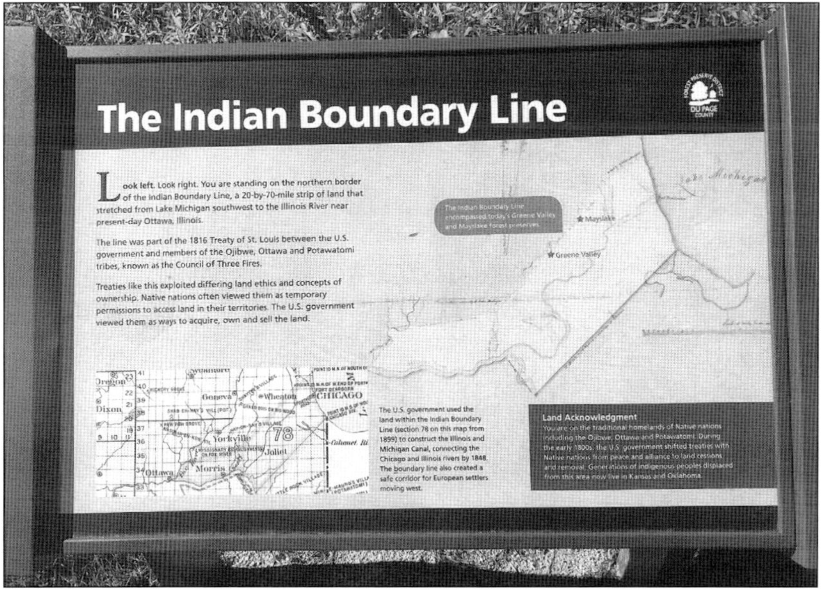

This is a sign at the entrance to the Greene Valley Forest Preserve, which stretches from Hobson Road to the southern border of DuPage County. Concerned about the increasing population density and related developer greed, W.B. Greene envisioned open land with clear streams and fresh air for public use. He donated 100 acres of the Greene farm plus an equivalent tract, including Oak Cottage and the Greene barn, at a bargain price to the Forest Preserve District of DuPage County, which it accepted. He also negotiated with several farmers in the valley who had ceased farming to add their acreage to this initial donation. The assembled property was named the Greene Valley Forest Preserve. Consequently, far more acreage than just the Greene farm was protected for public use. The balance of the farm (west of Greene Road) was sold to a developer on a long-term contract. (Photograph by the author.)

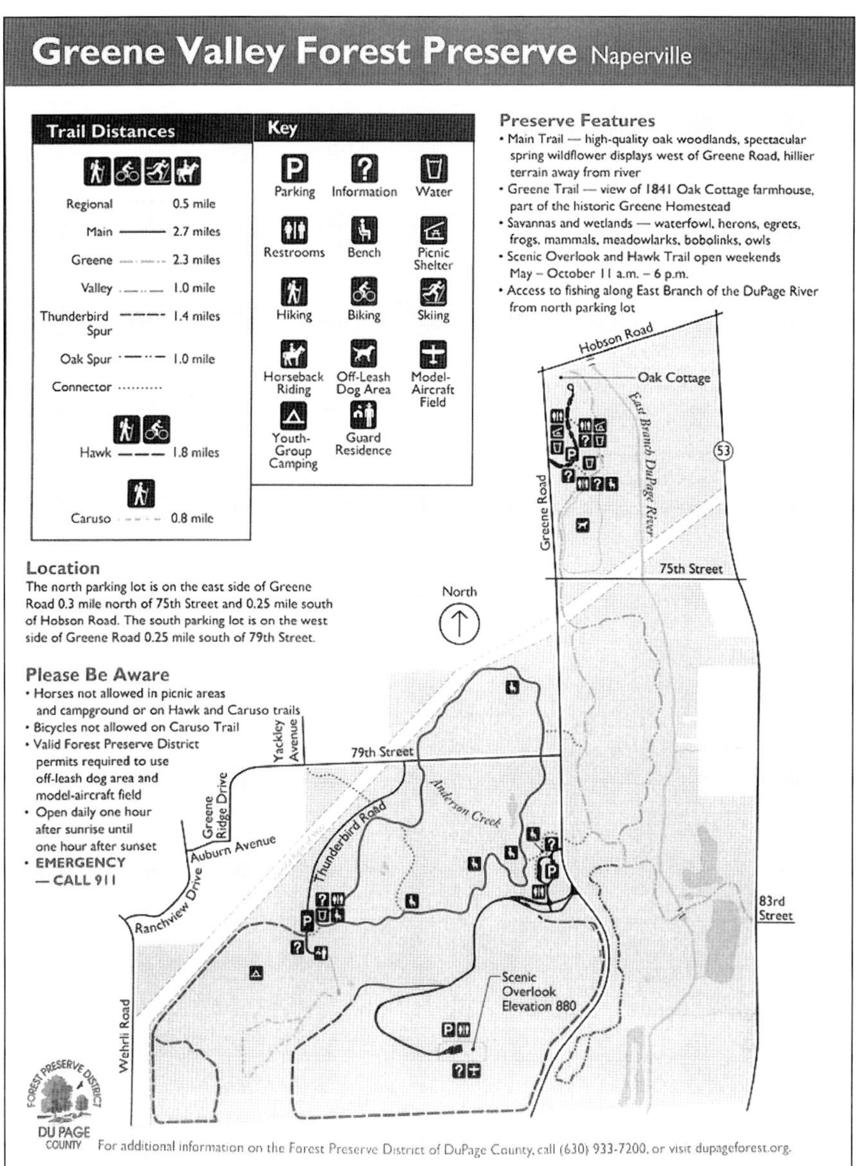

This is a map of the Greene Valley Forest Preserve, a 1,388-acre legacy left behind by William Bertram Greene as a contribution to future generations. The historical Greene family homestead with Oak Cottage and the barn, which had sheltered six generations, is at the northern end of the preserve. The preserve gives visitors a glimpse of the balanced ecosystem that was present more than a century ago. Greene Valley with its high-quality oak woodlands, savannahs, and meadows with more than 540 native plant species is a botanist's paradise. It is also home to a vast variety of wildlife such as frogs, waterfowl, egrets, herons, coyotes, and wolves. The preserve offers 12 miles of trails, picnic spots, a youth campground, and more. The scenic overlook is the highest nonstructural point in metropolitan Chicago and sits atop a former landfill that still produces methane gas, which is captured and converted to electrical energy serving about 7,500 homes. The hope is that the special qualities of this place of nature and of people will not be taken for granted and that its heritage will be protected, preserved, and honored for generations to come. (Photograph by the author.)